STANLEY BALDWIN

and the Search for Consensus

DUNCAN WATTS

Hodder & Stoughton

A MEMBER OF THE HODDER HEADLINE GROUP

Acknowledgements

The publishers would like to thank the following to reproduce copyright illustrations in this volume:

Popperfoto, cover illustration; Bodleian Library p.79; *Daily Express*/Centre for the Study of Cartoon and Caricature, University of Kent at Canterbury pp.68, 127; Hulton Getty p.93; Punch Publications pp.58, 131.

From the author
To Jill and the family

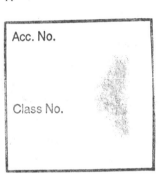
British Library Cataloguing in Publication Data

Watts, Duncan
  Stanley Baldwin and the Search for Consensus. –
  (Personalities and Powers)
  1. Baldwin of Bewdley, Stanley Baldwin, Earl, 1867–1947
  2. Conservative Party 3. Great Britain – Politics and government –
  1910–1936 4. Great Britain – Politics and government – 1936–45
  I. Title
  941'.083'092

ISBN 0 340 65843 6

First published 1996
Impression number 10 9 8 7 6 5 4 3 2 1
                     1999 1998 1997 1996

Typeset by Business Color Print Ltd, Welshpool, Powys, Wales.
Printed in Great Britain for Hodder & Stoughton Educational,
a division of Hodder Headline Plc, 338 Euston Road, London NW1 3BH
by Redwood Books, Trowbridge, Wiltshire.

CONTENTS

INTRODUCTION

Stanley Baldwin was the dominant politician of the inter-war years. No other prime minister of the twentieth century has held the highest office for three non-consecutive terms. Yet for all his longevity at the top, his popularity and his predominance over an era, his career has rarely since been held in high esteem and his personality remains something of an enigma.

In such a long political innings, Baldwin was inevitably confronted by many difficult problems and challenges. If he was unable to solve some of them or foresee the dangers which his generation faced at home and abroad, he was not alone in these shortcomings. Inter-war Britain was not a period of great leaders. Lloyd George was out of fashion, vehemently attacked by Baldwin as a 'great dynamic force . . . a very terrible thing', words which, as A. J. P. Taylor put it, 'announced the spirit of his own future conduct'. When Lloyd George fell, the dynamic days were over and the period after 1922 was to be, in the words of Mowat, 'the rule of the pygmies'. He remained in public life, and 'stonily watched the country sink into the hopeless morass of depression and unemployment, while lesser men frittered away Britain's power in the world'. He never returned to office and Winston Churchill, the other big personality of the era, spent much of the time in the political wilderness.

Baldwin was one of the men usually portrayed as being of lesser calibre, and it is true that he never gave the country great leadership. That which he did give was not noticeably inferior to that of Balfour or Asquith and many other premiers who have led their party and their country. He was, as Roy Jenkins observes in his biography, 'unlucky in having to engage at the end of his career with major events to the handling of which his talents were ill-suited'. This engagement 'cannot be held to enhance his reputation. It should not be allowed to destroy it'.

In the 1930s, Baldwin had been a senior Cabinet Minister and Prime Minister at a time when the rise of the European dictators posed a potentially formidable threat to the prospects for peace on the continent. In 1940 he was blamed for Britain's lack of military preparedness, and the attacks upon him were often surprisingly venomous. These issues need to be borne in mind in any final assessment of Baldwin's contribution. But in seeking to resurrect his reputation from the disfavour into which it fell the historian can dwell upon positive, if less dramatic, qualities than those possessed by the political giants of the era.

THE PEOPLE'S MAN

As a parliamentarian, Stanley Baldwin kept his self-control and never lost his temper; he was one of the most courteous debaters the House has ever produced. The generosity he grafted onto Britain's political tradition enjoyed wide support from the electorate, who for the most part trusted him. They liked his style and warmed to his simple eloquence as he spoke in 1925 of 'The sounds of England, the tinkle of the hammer on the anvil in the country smithy, the corncrake on a dewy morning, the sound of the scythe against the whetstone, and the sight of a plough team coming over the brow of a hill . . .' He loved the enduring things of English life, the country's history, its traditions and its countryside. Above all, he admired its people whose virtues he was wont to extol: 'kindliness, sympathy with the underdog, love of home – are not these all characteristics of the ordinary Englishman that you know? He has a strong individualism in this, that he doesn't want to mould himself into any common mould, to be like everybody else. He likes to develop his own individuality'. He had an intuitive understanding of the English character, and he represented what one speaker has called 'the warmer and deeper instincts of provincial England'. He knew, or believed he knew, what the English people, especially the middle and professional classes, would like, and felt comfortable in meeting their needs. Not for nothing is he sometimes referred to as 'God's Englishman', for he sounded the part and he and his wife both looked appropriate for the role as well.

Baldwin was able to project himself as straightforward, unsophisticated and unambitious, though in truth he was a more professional operator than was immediately apparent; the simplicity could be deceptive. Yet for all of his guile and artfulness, he remained obstinately likeable, the sort of Englishman with whom many people could feel at ease. Moreover, he was a man of moral decency: 'There is nothing else for this generation to do than devote itself as no other generation has done in the past to the betterment of its millions of people who have not had our advantages.' He was able to obtain people's respect (if not always that of his own party) without standing on his dignity, determined to the last to be conciliatory. His eminent reasonableness and transparent honesty earned him the trust of many trade unionists, and enabled him to deal successfully with the General Strike even if bitterness lingered on for some while after.

Baldwin may not have been very energetic in seeking the fulfilment of his principles, but he was a man who preached Christian virtues and a simple patriotism. Above all, he set out to create and maintain a sense of national unity. His was an uncomplicated philosophy of life, for he was a man of peace at home and abroad, who emphasised four key attributes – 'faith, hope, love and work'. He had moderate, non-confrontational attitudes, and if he favoured tranquillity it was not just because of the lack of energy which he often exhibited. It was also because he was a man of the consensus, who genuinely believed that the quiet and reasonable pursuit of compromise was the best way forward. Not for him the drama of posturing and partisanship, for 'no Party is on the whole better than another . . . no creed does more than shadow imperfectly forth some one side of truth'.

As Prime Minister, Baldwin disliked economic and military matters and made little attempt to master such subjects before a Cabinet meeting. If the matter under discussion proved uninteresting he would go to sleep, or pretend to do so, and only intervene if the debate threatened to drag on without a positive result. Sir John Simon, a leading Liberal who worked alongside Baldwin in the National Government after 1931, knew him well and was in a good position to assess his performance at first hand. He recognised his strengths, but also his lack of leadership:

Stanley Baldwin was the typical Englishman, the embodiment of English ways, devoted to the English tradition above everything else in the world. His course was guided more by instinct than by any elaborate process of reasoning and his instinct usually led him to the conclusion which the ordinary man approved.

... His method was to ask what I proposed and then, after a series of grimaces as he pulled in silence at his pipe, to say, 'Well, carry on'.

Winston Churchill drew an interesting comparison between Neville Chamberlain and Baldwin. Both were men characteristic of the new Conservative Party, rich industrialists rather than aristocratic landowners, and each appreciated that Britain's greatness depended on industrial strength and the size of its exports. But whereas Chamberlain was concerned to master the details, not just a few obvious facts, Baldwin made no pretence to impress his colleagues with detailed knowledge. Yet what he lacked in preparation, he made up for by his understanding of people and the way they operated. Baldwin was the wiser, more comprehending person, but without detailed executive capacity. Indeed, he had a low concept of the Prime Minister's position, as is illustrated by his observation that it was like 'being stuck in a gluepot' and also that 'His Majesty's ministers are co-equal'.

Baldwin had a sense of proportion and was able to keep his Cabinet in order not by personal ascendancy but because, on those issues in which he was interested, he was able to speak for a wider constituency than many of them. He did not claim to know all the answers, as the exchange of comments in one Cabinet meeting indicates. Austen Chamberlain, Churchill and Baldwin were in discussion:

AC to WC: 'I am entirely with you on this.'
WC: 'I am not entirely with myself.'
SB: 'How well I know that feeling.'

He conceded that he was not an intellectual; indeed, he rather despised such men. As he put it in his speech at Plymouth in 1923, 'I am not a clever man. I know nothing of political tactics.' He went on to speak of his wish to do the 'honest and right thing'. However, his modesty was perhaps overdone, for though few could dispute his lack of intellect there was no doubt that he excelled in the art of political tactics. He was a wily general, and though his strategy sometimes went awry, his tactics were usually masterly. He knew the value of evoking the picture of a self-deprecating, modest countryman, an old-fashioned industrialist who had greatness thrust upon him. It led people to underestimate him. In fact he was a skilled operator, and as such was not just a popular figure in the country but very much a politician's politician.

Baldwin was very conscious of the way he looked and sounded. He was careful to ensure how he was photographed and knew from which side he needed to be taken to convey the best demeanour. In private, he practised his gestures to ensure that they created a favourable impression, for he well understood that the picture of a relaxed gentleman, puffing on his pipe as he surveyed the English landscape, was well-attuned to what people wanted, and inspired their confidence. In the words of *The Times* correspondent in 1930: 'He cultivates the character of an amateur in politics to a point which is maddening to ardent politicians.'

Many of those who worked with him recognised a different picture to the one the public knew. They found him devious, at times ruthless. His Attorney-General, Sir Donald Somerville, spoke for a number of others when he remarked that: 'They talk of honest, stupid Stanley Baldwin; believe me, he is the most ruthless and astute politician of the day.' Churchill saw him as 'the greatest party manager the Conservatives ever had' and Lloyd George even went as far as to label him 'the most formidable antagonist I ever encountered'. However, by stressing the range of his extensive qualities, it did of course let some of them off the hook for being outplayed by him.

Baldwin was an excellent House of Commons man who spent much time there. He listened to debates, understanding the House intimately and knowing how to handle its moods. He was accessible to MPs, affable, could converse on cricket, farming and many other topics of interest to his colleagues. He understood the importance of getting the best out of men, and was prepared to invest time and effort to win their confidence. He succeeded, and many would have echoed Asquith's judgement that he was 'one of the nicest fellows in the House'.

Luck and good fortune also played their parts throughout Baldwin's career. He was born into a comfortable middle-class household, and inherited a fortune which ensured that he would always have financial security. He entered Parliament when his father died, inheriting from him the safe seat of Bewdley. He rose from obscurity as a backbencher and gained minor office in the First World War, largely because the Chancellor knew his father. He became Chancellor of the Exchequer in 1922 only because other potential candidates among the Conservatives were not then within the party fold, and after a more probable candidate had rejected the vacancy. He became leader and Prime Minister at a time when his only rival, Lord Curzon, suffered from obvious disadvantages. Having got to the top, fortune continued to smile on him and at key moments in his career he was able to exploit a favourable situation to his advantage, as at the time of the Abdication Crisis in 1936.

Baldwin undoubtedly recognised some of his own limitations for he was a modest man – 'no use to God or man' he once suggested in a throwaway line. He was surprised at his own success in attaining the leadership of his party. As he told Asquith: 'The position of leader came to me when I was inexperienced, before I was really fitted for it, by a succession of curious chances that could not have been foreseen. I had never expected it; I was in no way trained for it.'

Yet if Baldwin reached the premiership in a precipitate way, once he arrived in Downing Street he soon adjusted to the position. The Liberal *Daily News* noted as early as 1923 that:

> The office of Prime Minister fits Mr Baldwin like a glove . . . A man little known to the general public suddenly . . . is found to be entirely adequate to the exacting role. The remarkable evolution of Mr Baldwin's character and his rapid growth in authority is the outstanding feature of the Session.

AN INFLUENTIAL ENIGMA

In the following decade and a half, Baldwin came to symbolise the character of British political life between the wars, an era often remembered as 'the Baldwin era'. Fair-minded and decent, able to inspire confidence and trust, not lacking in courage – these were qualities which won him admiration. Luck and political skill sustained him in his long career. If he was not endowed with brilliant talent, he compensated for the deficiency by native common sense, abundant guile and a shrewd insight into how people thought and reacted.

The image he fostered was a clever one, for by appearing to be a simple countryman he was able to tap into a vein of nostalgia for an idyllic past and appeal to the basic patriotism of ordinary people. He seemed to embody those elements which made Britain respected for its attachment to civilised standards, at a time when in other parts of Europe those values were coming under threat.

Underneath the rustic exterior there was what Kenneth Young has called an 'inner tremulousness'. He was a deeply sensitive person, much given to nervousness on the big occasion, and never quite the master of his emotions as others might have believed. The contradictions in his character and the conflict between the public image and the private man make him a difficult person to fathom, and it is not surprising that one writer, Robert Pearce, should depict him as the 'Enigmatic Premier'.

The task in this short study is to seek to unravel some of the complexities of his personality and to come to a better understanding of 'what made him tick'. In so doing, the merits and deficiencies of his performance will hopefully be thrown into a sharper focus, so that we can see why he was on the one hand so dominant and so popular in the political life of the 1920s and '30s, but also so reviled in his later years.

HISTORIANS AND STANLEY BALDWIN

Political reputations come and go, and it is only in the last three decades that historians have attempted to restore one which was so besmirched in the years of war and in the post-1945 era.

Baldwin's role in the history of Britain between the wars was pivotal, and a knowledge of his person and approach is vital for anyone seeking to know and understand the period well. Historians have tended to agree on his importance, but have varied significantly in their assessment.

In his lifetime, Baldwin was the subject of a perceptive study by A. G. Whyte: *Stanley Baldwin; A Biographical Character Study* (1928). Wickham Steed's *The Real Stanley Baldwin* (1930) and Arthur Bryant's study to mark his retirement, *Stanley Baldwin* (1937), are also readable and interesting accounts, though written too early to have the benefit of hindsight and reflection. The five volumes of Baldwin's own speeches (published between 1926 and 1939) also provide an insight into his attitudes and priorities, and they read better than do many such compilations.

Baldwin did not write a volume of his own recollections of the 'Baldwin age', but relied instead on the labours of others. In 1944 he entrusted the task of producing an official biography to G. M. Young, who was to serve him badly. It was an unfortunate choice, though Baldwin was not to know that Young had already written (in 1940) an advance obituary which was hostile in its evaluation. Young was from the beginning unsympathetic to his subject. Baldwin was unable to explain himself convincingly to someone with whom there was no natural rapport, and Young saw Baldwin's reticence as evasiveness and did not respond well to his brief and sometimes unfinished asides.

In 1952, Young published his version of Baldwin's role in inter-war political life, *Stanley Baldwin*. As Lord Blake has commented, it was 'sketchy and inadequate', an altogether unsatisfactory study of the Conservative leader. A. J. P. Taylor similarly wrote that it treated Baldwin 'slightly and slightingly', but for a while there was nothing else available. Few of Baldwin's friends were able to leap to his defence, for most of them were dead, and so the charges against Baldwin remained for some while unanswered. Eventually in 1955, a response came from Baldwin's son, A. W. Baldwin, in *My Father: The True Story*. This attempted to redress the balance. It was an impressive response, but its objectivity was inevitably clouded by filial devotion.

It was not until 1969 that K. Middlemas and J. Barnes wrote their voluminous study, *Baldwin: A biography*. This was certainly comprehensive, and included a degree of detail which is difficult for any but the most devoted buff to master, but it tried with considerable success to redress the balance and present a fairer coverage.

Montgomery Hyde's *Baldwin, The Unexpected Prime Minister* (1973) is an interesting account by a professional political biographer, and Kenneth Young's *Baldwin*, published three years later, maintained the improvement in the quality of Baldwin literature. This latter is one of the most useful and vivid portrayals of its subject and presents some of the complexities of the man who dominated British politics for so long.

Finally, in 1987 Roy Jenkins, an accomplished biographer, produced *Baldwin*, a remarkably fair and balanced reappraisal. The book is elegantly written, as one would expect from such a source, authoritative and highly readable. However, it is targeted at a sophisticated audience more versed in twentieth-century history, and this perhaps makes it less accessible for those seeking a shorter account to facilitate their examination study.

1

EARLY LIFE AND CAREER

Stanley Baldwin was born on 3 August 1867 into a family of ironmasters. His ancestors had turned to the iron industry in the early days of the Industrial Revolution and made a success of it. Alfred, his father, represented the third generation and became the proprietor of the family firm. He rescued it from the threat of bankruptcy, extended its operations and turned it into a public company. The Baldwins became again a prosperous family with a substantial fortune.

The family boast was that they lived 'close to the works, among [their] own people', and Alfred prided himself on his knowledge of every worker's Christian name. He represented the decent paternalism of the better type of Victorian employer and his religious view of his responsibilities meant that he saw his work as something more than merely running a business – more of a sacred trust. He also felt that his energies should serve the wider community and he became a Worcestershire MP for 16 years (1892–1908) and Chairman of the Great Western Railway.

Mrs Baldwin, Stanley's mother, was of mixed Scottish Highland and Welsh stock. The daughter of a Wesleyan minister, she was born into a family where money was often lacking but artistic taste and intelligence were available in abundance. Her sisters made interesting marriages, one to the Victorian painter, Burne-Jones, another to Edward Poynter, also an artist and later President of the Royal Academy. Another sister married J. L. Kipling; Rudyard Kipling was Stanley Baldwin's first cousin.

Young Stanley was brought up in a wealthy and happy environment. His parents were affectionate and the atmosphere at home was warm and encouraging. Although he had no brothers or sisters, he was not short of cousins on both sides of his family. He was encouraged to develop his literary leanings and later recalled how, as a small boy, he was interested in books and spent his time 'reading all day in that most comfortable attitude, lying on his stomach on the hearthrug in front of the fire'. He knew *Pilgrim's Progress* by heart, he was captivated by Dickens and made an early start on Shakespeare via *Lambs' Tales*.

Stanley was sent to a highly reputable preparatory school, Hawtrey's, near Slough, in the same term as his cousin, Ambrose Poynter. So began his private education. He was the first member of his family to receive a conventional upper-class training and he made good use of the initial experience. He was top of the class by the time he left, but he did not take the usual route from Hawtrey's to Eton. His father wished to split the two cousins and so instead he was sent to Harrow, which proved to be a most unfortunate choice.

His career at Harrow divided into two phases. At first he did well, winning academic prizes in History, Classics and Mathematics, and showing some prowess on the games field. However, he was later accused of writing pornography in lesson time, a prank viewed particularly seriously as the offending piece was to be sent to his cousin at Harrow's rival school, Eton. Dr Montagu Butler, the headmaster, was more concerned with the honour of the school than with any notion of justice, and without giving the boy any opportunity to explain his actions, he severely flogged him.

The nature of Baldwin's composition has remained unclear, but whatever its content, the offence was trivial in itself. The punishment seemed out of all proportion to what had been done. The headmaster never forgave him and placed no confidence or trust in him. He denied him the opportunity to become a monitor, without offering any explanation, an incident which only served to increase the mutual suspicion felt by each of them. For Baldwin, the 'pornography' episode left an indelible mark on his character. He objected to being given no chance to explain or protest, and thought his treatment arbitrary and unfair. Thereafter, he did much less well than had been expected. He lost interest, and became lazy and withdrawn, adopting what his main biographers, Middlemas and Barnes, have called a 'facade of well-intentioned stupidity'.

It was unfortunate that he met with the same austere headmaster in the next stage of his career. When he proceeded to Trinity College, Cambridge, he found that Dr Butler had been appointed as the new

Master and arrived one term later. The young Baldwin never showed much academic appetite and wasted a lot of time. Naturally indolent and reticent, he made little attempt to enter into any aspect of College life, and never spoke in debates as he had once been willing to do. He graduated in 1888 with a Third in History, and subsequently rarely spoke of his experiences at any of his places of learning.

He was later to claim that most of his knowledge was derived from experience in business, observation on railway journeys and through private reading. Nonetheless, he did recognise that he had frittered away his opportunities, and in 1924 felt able to admit that, 'If there is one thing more than any other of which I feel ashamed today, it is to think how I, with the chances I had in youth – and I venture to think with the capacity to take equal advantage of them – wasted so much time when I was at the University.' His father was aware that his son had wasted his talents, and after Stanley left Cambridge expressed the wish that 'I hope you won't get a Third in life'.

A BUSINESS CAREER

The young graduate contemplated a career in the Church, but without enthusiasm he decided on the family firm. He later told the House of Commons about the impact it made on him:

> It was a place where I knew and had known from childhood, every man on the ground . . . a place where I was able to talk to the men not only about the troubles in the works but troubles at home, and their wives. It was a place where strikes and lock-outs were unknown. It was a place where the fathers and grandfathers of the men then working there had worked, and where their sons went automatically into the business. It was also a place where nobody ever 'got the sack', and where we had a natural sympathy for those who were less concerned in efficiency than is this generation, and where a large number of old gentlemen used to spend their days sitting on wheelbarrows, smoking their pipes.

Baldwin was never to prove an enterprising businessman, and lacked the entrepreneurial qualities which his father had exhibited throughout his career. What did distinguish his attitude to the family business was his willingness to work hard, and to devote himself to maintaining the tradition of a sense of responsibility to those who worked within it. He got on well with ordinary people, and took pride in ensuring that they were content with their conditions. He developed other skills, and his ability to read a balance-sheet and his mastery of the firm's financial position made him a useful partner for his father.

His ability to adapt to his responsibilities surprised many close to him, for they knew that he initially found the routine of daily work uncongenial and often grumbled about its dullness. His cousin, Harold, noted the way in which Stanley adjusted to his role and remarked that: 'He is quite the man of business when in office, but once outside, the same dear merry soul he has ever been.' He seemed to have found personal satisfaction, and his immersion in factory life kept him sufficiently busy to stop him from lapsing for too long into the reflective, introspective moods to which he had sometimes been prone.

Baldwin never possessed any ambition to make more money just for the sake of so doing, and as a man of substance, felt that he should make a contribution to the wider community. He became the chairman of a board of school managers, a Worcestershire county councillor and a Justice of the Peace, but despite such involvement, he was never hardworking and his record of service was an undistinguished one. He enjoyed his holidays and after his marriage in 1892 he often took a month off to travel in Europe. In January, he and his wife were normally to be found with the Kiplings, skiing in one of the Alpine winter sports centres. He liked Europe and Europeans; he may have later been viewed as a typical Englishman, but he was not an insular one. He knew the pre-1914 continent well, he was fluent in French and could speak sufficient German to hold a reasonable conversation.

INTO POLITICS

Baldwin's father had been the Tory MP for Bewdley in Worcestershire since 1892, and though he did not make any advancement on the parliamentary ladder he acquitted himself well and was respected as a successful businessman and shrewd backbencher. The young Baldwin met many of his father's political friends, and was involved in constituency work, attending meetings and canvassing at election time.

He often attended gatherings of the Primrose League, an organisation founded after Disraeli's death as a way of perpetuating his memory and maintaining the tradition of 'One Nation' Conservatism.

In 1906 Baldwin made his first unsuccessful bid to enter the House of Commons as the candidate for Kidderminster, and for a while there was a possibility of father and son acting as representatives of neighbouring constituencies. It did not materialise. In the Liberal landslide victory of that year, Kidderminster was lost even though the influence of the Chamberlain family in the Midlands mitigated the severity of the anti-Unionist tide in the region.

Joseph Chamberlain used his influence to try to secure a vacant candidacy for Baldwin after his defeat, but the attempt failed and prospects of a seat in the House began to fade for no election was due until 1913. Baldwin wondered whether the opportunity had passed, and was saddened to have dashed his father's hopes. However, after the sudden death of Alfred Baldwin, his son was chosen to fight the seat in his place. In 1908, at the age of 40, Stanley Baldwin became the MP for the western division of Worcestershire which became re-drawn as Bewdley. He remained its MP until his elevation to the peerage in 1937.

There was little indication of any ambition on Baldwin's part. He was an undistinguished backbencher who made little impact on the House. He rarely spoke (five times only in the years before 1914), though his occasional utterances were generally well received. It was appreciated by many MPs that he had a good understanding of the business community. He was considered to be a safe and loyal party man, well-respected but little known. Lord Edmund Talbot's summary was an indication of how he was viewed by many Tory MPs: 'He was discreet enough to be safe and stupid enough not to intrigue.'

Baldwin enjoyed his political life, and found it provided him with greater fulfilment than he had experienced before. He shunned any involvement in party coteries, but was liked by many colleagues, and by many on the opposing side. In the words of one contemporary Liberal: 'Most of us knew him as a private member who attended with great regularity, who was exceedingly friendly to many of us, without any distinction of Party, and who took a keen and lively interest in the lives and affairs of many members.' His reputation as a fair-minded, affable and tolerant MP in those early days in Parliament was eventually to stand him in good stead in future controversies. But at the time he was often uncertain of his abilities, his manner was diffident and he did not urge his own claims.

It looked as though he was unlikely to advance, for Baldwin gave the impression of lacking ambition and he had not made a striking impression as a man of talent or outstanding ability. In the First World War, he was too old to fight but neither did he at first feel able to make a worthwhile political contribution. Then, in 1916, he was plucked from relative obscurity to be Parliamentary Private Secretary to Bonar Law, the Unionist leader and Chancellor of the Exchequer. It was the first rung on the ladder, but the appointment was viewed by many MPs as a reward for loyal service rather than as a springboard for future advancement.

GOVERNMENT OFFICE

In 1917, Stanley Baldwin became Financial Secretary to the Treasury, his first government post. According to A. J. P. Taylor, this was largely in order to do the Treasury entertaining which Law disliked. However, the fact that Baldwin was appointed probably owed more to the force of family connections between the Laws and the Baldwins, for Bonar Law had felt a deep respect for his father's abilities.

Baldwin proved to be an able choice for a post that suited him well. At that time, it required him to act as deputy for the Leader of the House, but the main task was to conduct much of the administrative work of the Chancellor of the Exchequer who laid down the broad lines of departmental policy but did not greatly involve himself in planning its implementation. Though not deeply impressed with his work, nor politically close to him, Law recognised that he was a competent assistant who might proceed further up the ministerial ladder. But to most observers Baldwin displayed more talent than his Chancellor acknowledged. He was effective in debates, and proved skilful in handling difficult issues. His performances became increasingly confident, and he became adept at declining requests for policy changes in a way that left fellow MPs unhurt by the refusal. Middlemas and Barnes note how Baldwin was building up a 'solid warmth of feeling' by his personal attributes:

Reasonableness, patience, good-humoured tolerance – qualities which rarely filter through the opaque medium of the lobby into the national press . . . He had already learnt the most difficult art of giving way gracefully and, even better, of resisting the temptation to make political capital out of the concession.

It was in his new office that Baldwin made a gesture which has been the point of some discussion. He gave a part of his personal fortune to the Treasury, a righteous if ultimately ineffective move. The decision reflected his strong feeling that those who had benefited during the war should make a personal sacrifice on behalf of those who had suffered family loss. As a young man, he had held a commission in the Volunteers, but he was too old to serve in the forces when war broke out in 1914.

The suffering of the four years to 1918 made a deep mark on him, and his later unwillingness to contemplate the possibility of another war was due to his horror at the bloodshed in the Great War. He spoke with feeling of 'a lost generation' and he felt that those who had stayed at home, and in some cases had flourished in those years, owed a debt to society. Others suffered family losses and made sacrifices of a sort that he was unable to make. Whilst his wife was energetic in voluntary work, he showed generosity in his charitable giving. Money was given to local hospitals, and for the duration of the war he paid the contributions of every serviceman in his constituency to Friendly Societies, to ensure their family's entitlement to health care.

In 1919, another personal gesture would go some way to relieve his conscience as well as contribute to the country's financial solvency at a time when the National Debt was very high. He used 20 per cent of his fortune to buy war loan stock and then handed it back to the Treasury for cancellation. He explained his action in a letter to *The Times* in 1919 which he did not sign in his own name. The initials FST should have given the game away – which, from the style and tone of the wording, may have been what he wanted – but it was some considerable while before the identity of the author was realised.

Baldwin began his letter by referring to the way in which the British people had rallied in 1914, and describing the different crisis faced by the nation now that peace had returned. He continued:

How can the nation be made to understand the gravity of the financial situation; that love of country is better than love of money? This can be done only by example, and the wealthy classes have today an opportunity of service which can never recur. They know the danger of the present debt; they know the weight of it in the years to come. They know the practical difficulties of a universal statutory capital levy. Let them impose upon themselves, each as he is able, a voluntary levy. It should be possible to pay to the Exchequer within twelve months such a sum as would save the taxpayer 50 millions a year. I have been considering the matter for nearly two years, but my mind moves slowly; I dislike publicity, and I hoped that someone else might lead the way. I have made as accurate an estimate as I am able of the value of my own estate and have arrived at a total of about £580,000. I have decided to realise 20 per cent of that amount or, say, £120,000 which will purchase £150,000 of the new War Loan and present it to the government for cancellation. I give this portion of my estate as a thank-offering in the firm conviction that never again shall we have such a chance of giving our country that form of help which is so vital at the present time.

Yours etc.

FST

THE PRESIDENCY OF THE BOARD OF TRADE, 1921–22

During the governmental reshuffle in 1921, when Bonar Law resigned the party leadership on grounds of ill-health, Lloyd George offered Baldwin the position of President of the Board of Trade, a Cabinet post. Law advised him to get rid of his one defect, his excessive modesty, as soon as possible, and Baldwin accepted the advancement. He quickly found himself plunged into a difficult industrial dispute in the mining industry.

Miners were objecting to the moves being made to deregulate the mines which had been controlled by the government during the war. By late 1920, the owners found themselves back in control of their pits, and had to cope with the problems of foreign competition at a time of low demand for coal. Many mines were near-bankrupt, others were in need of urgent modernisation if they were to be economically viable. The response of the owners was to argue that, at a time of falling profits, they could no longer pay wartime wages. Miners were exasperated, for they had seen nationalisation as a possible outcome of post-war reconstruction, and now felt embittered that private ownership was leaving them exposed.

There was little hope of industrial peace in the mining industry, and talk of wage cuts and strike action was in the air when Baldwin took over at the Board of Trade. Fortunately for him, Lloyd George played the leading role in the discussions with the miners, and though Baldwin was present he said little. The threat of a general strike was averted when the unity of the Triple Alliance of the miners, the railwaymen and the transport workers cracked. Lloyd George, supported by Baldwin, offered a subsidy to the mine owners to enable them to make a better offer to the miners, and this was eventually accepted.

Black Friday was the name given to the day (15 April 1921) on which the partnership of the three unions had broken down. But the miners had gained something from their action, including for the first time a national agreement on wage levels. The owners, however, were unhappy with a settlement which they had been under pressure to concede, and four years later were to seek to reverse the principles which had been agreed for the just fixing of wage and profit levels. Then, it would be Baldwin as Prime Minister who had to deal with the problem. For now, as President of the Board of Trade, Baldwin's role in the eventual outcome was a small and indecisive one. He was content to take a back seat in the negotiations and watch Lloyd George in action, as the Prime Minister exhibited his subtle negotiations tactics.

During his presidency Baldwin was involved in piloting a Bill through the House which provided for the safeguarding of new and fragile industries, a measure which had been drawn up by his predecessor and for which he had no great enthusiasm. He could accept that some measure of protection for infant companies might be necessary for they might be unable to withstand foreign competition. On the whole, however, the bent of his thinking was against protectionism, for he believed that the only answer to industrial weakness lay in a general revival of European trade.

As President of the Board of Trade, Baldwin was a popular minister. Businessmen liked him for they regarded him as 'one of us'. He listened to their anxieties with patience and good humour, and did his best to allay their fears by providing a clear answer to their questions. He was less effective in Cabinet, where he spoke little; as Wickham Steed (*The Real Stanley Baldwin*, 1930) observed, it was difficult to know whether this was because he was ruminating or merely inarticulate.

THE BREAK-UP OF THE COALITION

At the end of the war, the parties in the Coalition Government had continued their cooperation in order to handle the problems of demobilisation and reconstruction. There was a pact between Conservatives and Lloyd George's Liberals not to oppose each other and to fight on an agreed programme. The Coalition was to continue until 1922, but by then it was increasingly unpopular among rank and file Conservatives and caused an open row between the chairman of the party organisation and its leader, Austen Chamberlain.

Several aspects of Coalition policy were distasteful to Conservatives, notably the conduct of economic policy and the Irish settlement. Above all, however, there was a strong personal dislike and distrust of Lloyd George and his autocratic style of leadership. Too often he ignored the conventional methods of running a government and one of his own innovations, the sale of honours, was seen as particularly disreputable.

Conservative discontent also focused on Lloyd George's handling of the Chanak Crisis. The Turkish Empire had been destroyed during the First World War but after the cessation of hostilities only the Turks themselves had not won independence. Mustapha Kemal's national revolution in Turkey (1920) had been successful and after a drive against the Greeks who had been encroaching on their country, the Turks found themselves approaching British lines at Chanak, near Troy. Determined to resist aggression – or hoping to recreate a tide of jingoistic sentiment from which his government's popularity might benefit – Lloyd George threatened the Turks with the might of the British Empire if they continued to advance. The incident passed without conflict, but there was a surge of war-weary disapproval among many Conservatives which helped precipitate the events that toppled Lloyd George from office.

The Prime Minister continued to receive support from most of the abler Conservatives, but the Foreign Secretary, Lloyd Curzon, resigned. Party discontent on the backbenches and in the country was strong and these feelings were well represented by Stanley Baldwin. He became critical of the direction of policy in several areas, and he particularly disliked the tendency of 'LG' to conduct policies on the basis of the search for his personal advantage and popularity. Of the Chanak episode, he remarked that: 'We should never have got into such a mess.' He was appalled at the behaviour of some of his ministerial colleagues, such as Churchill, whom he believed to be a warmonger. He had, so he claimed, 'found out that W. and LG had been all for war and had schemed to make this country go to war with Turkey so that they should have a 'Christian' war v the Mahomedan and turn the Turks out of Europe. On the strength of that, they would call a general election at once and go to the country which, they calculated, would return them to office for another period of years.'

By the end of autumn 1922, Baldwin was convinced that the Conservatives must detach themselves from the Coalition. There may have been an element of self-interest in his thinking, as he calculated (in G. M. Young's words) 'how many steps were between him and the highest place'. On one occasion, he did announce that he would like to be Chancellor of the Exchequer: 'That is the limit of my ambitions.' Under Lloyd George, he did not expect to rise to that eminence. But Baldwin was also genuinely fearful of the damage which continuation of the Coalition would do to the Conservative Party and to British political life. When Austen Chamberlain suggested to Conservatives in the Cabinet that they should affirm their decision to fight the next election as Coalition partners once more, Baldwin was unhappy and showed his dissent.

By his own account to his wife, Baldwin behaved with some courage in making his disapproval clear, for at first no one else expressed a similar view. At a meeting with fellow ministers, he went as far as to say that 'I could not serve under LG again.' He suspected that this would be a serious blow to his career, and that the rest ' will follow LG, and I can't, so it means that I shall drop out of politics altogether'. He was much criticised by some of his fellows, and Churchill was amazed that such a relatively unknown figure should make a personal stand against the Prime Minister.

Nonetheless, there was an indication at the next gathering that a few others shared his misgivings, including the Chief Whip. He and the Party Chairman wanted a chance to air the topic, and they were looking for a leader around whose stand they could rally. Baldwin lacked the political stature, and it was Bonar Law on whom they placed their hopes. Law was under much pressure from Baldwin and the others, and his reluctance to challenge Chamberlain gradually broke down. Chamberlain decided on a party meeting to 'flush out the malcontents', and was confident that he would win; he told Birkenhead that the rebels 'must either follow our advice or do without us, in which case they must find their own Chief, and form a government at once. They would be in a damned fix!' A meeting was called at the Carlton Club (19 October 1922) to discuss the continuation of the Coalition, and Baldwin carefully prepared the ground for that meeting.

The crucial element in the events leading to the Conservative withdrawal from the Lloyd George Coalition was the decision of Bonar Law to join the rebels. He was reluctantly persuaded that the revolt of the rank and file was such that cooperation between the two parties was no longer possible. At the Carlton meeting, he urged the party to fight the next election as an independent Conservative Party. But the person who made the most telling speech was Baldwin, who took up a reference by a previous speaker to the value of Lloyd George as a dynamic leader:

> The Prime Minister was described this morning in *The Times*, in the words of a distinguished aristocrat, as a live wire. He was described to me, and to others, in more stately language, by the Lord Chancellor, as a dynamic force, and I accept these words. He is a dynamic force, and it is from that very fact that our troubles, in our opinion, arise. A dynamic force is a very terrible thing; it can crush you, but it is not necessarily right.
>
> It is owing to that dynamic force, and that remarkable personality, that the Liberal Party, to which he formerly belonged, has been smashed to pieces; and it is my firm conviction that, in time, the same thing will happen to our party . .

It was a brief, twelve-minute speech, but in its impact it was devastating. It precisely articulated the fears of many party members, as was evident from the reaction to his remarks. Bonar Law's voice was a more influential one and came later in the meeting, but it was Baldwin's which was such a revelation. In the words of one biographer, it exhibited 'a new eloquence; direct, conversational, monosyllabic; rising and falling without strain or effort between the homeliest humour and the most moving appeal'.

Many influential Conservatives had been committed to the Coalition, and their leader, Chamberlain, had even flirted with the idea of fusion (the creation of a single party). They wanted to fight the election as partners of the Liberals. However, in the vote at the close of the session, the Coalitionists were defeated by a majority of two to one.

THE BONAR LAW ADMINISTRATION, 1922–23

1922 has been regarded as a sufficiently auspicious date in Conservative history for it to provide the title for the present-day committee of party backbenchers. For Baldwin, it meant a further promotion. When Lloyd George resigned shortly after the Carlton Club meeting, Bonar Law headed a Conservative administration with Curzon again at the Foreign Office and Baldwin as the new Chancellor of the Exchequer.

The new Prime Minister quickly called an election, and Baldwin was active in the campaign. On one occasion, he drew a contrast between the characters of the old and the new premier, and observed that Lloyd George had once described Bonar Law as 'honest to the verge of simplicity'. He went on to express the reaction of the electorate: 'By God, that is what we have been looking for.'

During campaigning, Law pledged that 'this Parliament will not make any fundamental change in the fiscal system of this country' – an observation which was to cause problems for Baldwin in the future. At the time, it helped to preserve a degree of unity in the ruling councils of the party, and it went down well in the country for free trade was still the prevailing orthodoxy to which most people were attached. Baldwin himself confined his financial pledges to securing maximum economy in government expenditure, and to repayment of the American debt 'to the last penny'.

The Conservatives won a handsome victory, gaining a majority of more than 70. Law's stand on free trade played little part in the outcome, though *The Economist* noted that it enabled the voters of Lancashire, traditionally an area opposed to protection, to support the Tories with a clear conscience. For most electors, disillusion with the failure of the Coalition to handle post-war problems more effectively was the main cause of the Conservative victory. Liberals of any variety fared badly, and of the 56 National Liberals opposed by independent Conservatives, only two were successful.

Bonar Law had promised 'tranquillity and freedom from adventures and commitments both at home and abroad'. He was as good as his word, and in accordance with his pledges, the brief government which he led did very little. Its main achievement was the responsibility of Lord Curzon, who was successful in his bid to restore Anglo-Turkish relations (damaged by the Chanak Crisis) and resolve the diplomatic dispute between Turkey and Greece. At the Conference of Lausanne in 1923 he secured both of his objectives.

The other main item on the agenda was repayment of the American loan which was Baldwin's first priority as Chancellor. At an early stage in the war, the American government had financed the allies' purchase of war materials in the USA. This was done by issuing bonds, and by the end of hostilities the British government realised that the Americans could call for immediate repayment on conditions of their own choosing. Negotiations continued throughout 1919–20, but it was evident that there was no chance that the USA would repudiate the loans as the British government had hoped. Bonar Law believed that all allied war debts should have been written off, but, failing this, he considered that Britain should only pay the Americans the equivalent of what it had received from its debtors.

Baldwin, as Financial Secretary at the Treasury, would have been aware of the earlier negotiations, but he was not involved in them. As Chancellor of the Exchequer, however, it was his task to go to Washington with the Governor of the Bank of England, Montagu Norman, to discuss terms with the Americans. He anticipated a 'ghastly time', and the negotiations were marked by much wrangling. On his return, he was met at Southampton by journalists who asked about the meetings he had held, and Baldwin unwisely announced the terms which had been provisionally agreed and which he would commend to the Cabinet. He made it clear that, in his view, rejection would be out of the question, for the Americans would accept nothing less.

The settlement Baldwin had reached relieved Britain of one-third of its liability, though the Treasury had never expected to be asked to pay the whole sum. Of the agreed outstanding sum of £978,000,000, £34,000,000 would be paid annually for ten years (including three per cent interest), and £40,000,000 for a further 52 years (at three and a half per cent). In Cabinet, his colleagues were generally agreed that rejection would endanger the amity of the Anglo-American relationship and discourage the Americans from playing a further role in the reconstruction of post-war Europe. Opinion in the City of London and in the Treasury broadly concurred with the majority Cabinet opinion, but Bonar Law was very unhappy both with the terms themselves and the way in which Baldwin had bounced his colleagues into agreeing with his view by disclosing the deal and his own judgement upon it at

Southampton. At a Cabinet meeting in late January 1923, Bonar Law threatened resignation and when discussion was adjourned he wrote a letter to *The Times* attacking Baldwin's approach; using the pseudonym 'A Colonial', he reiterated his main arguments. It did not work, for he was faced with near unanimity in Cabinet. He backed down and Baldwin got his way – one of the few occasions when a prime minister has been so clearly overruled by his ministers.

The argument over the merits of the loan terms continued for several years. Baldwin's defenders pointed out that good relations with America were maintained and that as the decade unfolded US governments were willing to play an increasing role in European affairs – in particular, aiding German economic recovery with the Dawes Plan of 1924 and the Young Plan of 1929. Whether such help would have been forthcoming in any case is unclear. John Maynard Keynes, the economist, took the view that Baldwin overstressed the weakness of Britain's negotiating position. He told Baldwin's Private Secretary that 'It is the debtor who has the last word in these cases.' Certainly the French and the Italians were less amenable to American pressure, and held out for better terms for the resolution of their debt repayments.

During this episode the relationship between Baldwin and Bonar Law was placed under considerable strain, and the Chancellor ceased to call in at his next door neighbour's house in Downing Street every morning, as had been his custom. Law believed that Baldwin's behaviour over the war debts indicated his lack of experience. It troubled him that when the time came for him to retire (which could not be far off, given his declining health), the party had a limited choice for the succession. The Tories seemed to be woefully short of talent, for key personnel were absent from the government; Curzon apart, there was no one of front-rank status.

It was this absence of calibre which prompted Law to try to persuade Austen Chamberlain to join the government, with a view to succeeding him as leader. Chamberlain declined, for he knew that in the eyes of many Conservatives he would always remain suspect, as the man who was prepared to abandon the traditional independence of the party. The succession was unlikely to be his, and in any case he had a low view of the ministerial team and was unenthusiastic about serving as part of it. He had no reason to feel much enthusiasm for Baldwin, after his role in the Carlton Club meeting; he noted that he 'had the reputation, both in business and in the Treasury, of being unable to take a decision'.

As Chancellor of the Exchequer, Baldwin inevitably spent much of his time preparing for the Budget of April 1923. When his only Budget Speech was delivered, MPs were pleased to note its unusual brevity, and his performance was widely admired in the House. There was some surprise at the humour and lightness of tone, but this did not stop those present from taking the contents seriously. Baldwin was showing that he had hitherto unsuspected gifts, and both within the House and outside he was winning friends. Yet in the spring of 1923, as they listened to his remarks, few present would have suspected that they were listening to the man who as party leader and Prime Minister would dominate the politics of the next 14 years. Those who did suspect that he had the necessary qualities to make it to the very top would have been surprised to realise just how soon he would reach his destination.

timeline		
	1867	Stanley Baldwin born at Bewdley, Worcestershire
	1892	Married
	1908	Became MP for Bewdley
	1916	Parliamentary Private Secretary to Bonar Law
	1917	Financial Secretary to the Treasury
	1919	Donation of 20 per cent of wealth to the Treasury
	1921–22	President of the Board of Trade
	1922	Fall of the Lloyd George Coalition
	1922–23	Chancellor of the Exchequer

Points to Consider

1) What indications were there in 1914 that Baldwin was a 'politician with a future'?
2) What was the impact of the First World War upon his approach to social issues?
3) What qualities made him a useful – if undistinguished – member of the Lloyd George Coalition?
4) What did Baldwin find so distasteful about the personality and policies of Lloyd George?
5) What light does his role in bringing about the fall of the Lloyd George Coalition shed upon his political qualities?

THE FIRST ADMINISTRATION AND DEFEAT, 1923–4

On several occasions Baldwin had deputised for Bonar Law in his absence, but in the spring of 1923 he took over during a Commons' debate when the Prime Minister's voice failed. Law was clearly unwell and rumours of imminent resignation abounded. The only thing which prevented him from taking an early decision was that he felt reluctant to make any recommendation over the choice of his successor. He knew that the choice lay between an inexperienced Chancellor of the Exchequer and an able, if flawed, Foreign Secretary.

BALDWIN VERSUS CURZON

On 19 May, the decision to resign was announced to the King, for by then Law realised that there was no possibility that he could prolong his premiership; he had cancer of the throat. The King's Private Secretary, Lord Stamfordham, asked Davidson, Law's Parliamentary Private Secretary, for the names of people who should be consulted over the succession, and invited him to give his own views as a well-informed backbencher. The ablest Conservatives were out of the running for the leadership. It was too soon for the party to unite behind anyone who had argued for the continuance of the Coalition, and so the choice of Birkenhead, Horne or Austen Chamberlain was out of the question.

The only real alternatives were the two men Law had in mind. Baldwin had had a stormy few months at the Exchequer, and had not shown himself to be as forceful a negotiator over the American loan as Law would have liked. The Prime Minister nonetheless preferred Baldwin, and saw him as a man more appropriate for the times. He would have liked to serve a few months longer to give his Chancellor more of a chance to show his parliamentary mettle. As it was, he suspected that it would be Lord Curzon, who had acquitted himself with some distinction at the Foreign Office, who landed the premiership.

Curzon was sparkling company, witty and eloquent, an ardent and accomplished lover who had married twice for beauty and money. Winston Churchill later captured some of his brilliance in his tribute to him: 'The morning was golden, the noon-time silver, the afternoon bronze, and the evening lead. But each was polished until it shone after its own fashion.' He was generously endowed with gifts of mind and spirit, and there is little doubt that he was the more able of the two rivals. Most Conservatives recognised his intellectual gifts, his powers of industry and his dedication to public service. Moreover, he had just scored a notable diplomatic triumph by his shrewd conduct of negotiations in Lausanne.

An MP at 27, a Privy Counsellor at 36 and Viceroy of India at 39, Curzon had had a glittering career. But his personal deficiencies ultimately told against him. He was deeply unpopular among senior Conservatives. Many found his haughty, over-bearing and arrogant qualities captured in an undergraduate rhyme composed by his Balliol contemporaries. It pointed to his exalted opinion of himself, as well as to the privileged ranks from which he came:

My name is George Nathaniel Curzon,
I am a most superior person,
My cheek is pink, my hair is sleek,
I dine at Blenheim once a week.

Senior Conservatives knew he would be difficult to work with, and moreover, they doubted his loyalty and integrity. Because of his tendency to let down those who had been promised his backing, he was referred to by Lord Beaverbrook as a 'political jumping Jack'.

However, there was a more significant factor than Curzon's personal failings and this had more to do with the democratic era into which the country had moved. In Queen Victoria's time, many prime ministers had led the government from the House of Lords, but no one had done so since the death of Lord Salisbury in 1902. Since then, the upper chamber had lost much of its influence in the Constitution, which made it more desirable for the Premier to be in the House of Commons where the key consideration of government business was carried out. Moreover, with Labour now a substantial force in the Commons but without any representation in the Lords, the choice of a peer would have been particularly inappropriate.

Faced with a difficult choice, Law declined to offer advice. His was an invidious position and he did not feel enthusiastic about either man. His preference was based as much on the alleged defects of Curzon as on any deep admiration for Baldwin. Sickness gave him an acceptable reason for reticence.

The King took informal soundings from people who claimed to know Law's preference. Lord Salisbury (the representative of a much respected influential Conservative family) suggested that the outgoing Prime Minister was 'disinclined to pass over Curzon', whereas Davidson took a contrary view. Indeed, a memorandum supporting the claims of Baldwin and said to reflect Law's thinking, was actually drafted by Davidson, a family friend of the Chancellor.

Balfour, as a one-time Prime Minister, was also consulted about Law's preference. He rose from his sick-bed to endorse Baldwin, a recommendation which had more to do with his own strong feelings than it did with insight into Law's state of mind. He stressed the unfairness of choosing Curzon; Labour MPs would have found the choice of someone whom they could not call to account quite unacceptable. He did not glow over Baldwin's gifts, and after noting the startling rapidity of his rise to prominence referred to his career as 'more or less uneventful, and without any signs of special gifts or exceptional ability'.

Baldwin was duly sent for and Curzon was staggered and appalled by the choice, referring to it as 'the greatest blow and slur upon me and my public career, now at its summit, that I could ever have received'. Nonetheless, he had sufficient good grace to propose Baldwin's election as Conservative leader. He managed to bring himself to itemise some of the merits which he possessed, and his turn of phrase was adequately fulsome for the occasion. He remained convinced, however, that he himself possessed superior abilities and had been passed over for 'a man of the utmost insignificance' whose only real advantage was 'the supreme and indispensable qualification' of not being a peer. He had been denied the ultimate prize he had coveted all his life. (In sending for Baldwin, a constitutional precedent was established. Conventions do not have the force of law, but it has now long been accepted as a clear convention that no member of the House of Lords can expect to become Prime Minister as long as he or she retains a peerage.)

Baldwin was appointed Prime Minister on 21 May 1923. A week later, he was formally elected as leader of his party following Curzon's nomination. He had had a relatively brief and undistinguished ministerial career, with only six years of experience in government, and two at Cabinet rank. If Bonar Law was (in Asquith's phrase) 'the unknown Prime Minister', Baldwin was certainly one of the most inexperienced when he took over. Yet he was to lead his party for 14 years and have a key influence over the fortunes of British governments for much of that period. As he became better known, he was to develop in political strength and resilience, and acquire a remarkable hold over the nation.

FORMING A CABINET

In choosing his new Cabinet, Baldwin was aware that few ministers would agree to work alongside pro-Coalitionists such as Birkenhead. For his part, Austen Chamberlain was still nursing his wounds after the events of October 1922 and was unwilling to become involved. But with an eye to reconciling the divergent elements of the Conservative Party, Baldwin appointed Austen's younger brother, Neville, to the Chancellor.

Neville had entered the House of Commons in 1918, having like his father been Lord Mayor of Birmingham. In a brief spell as Director of National Service under Lloyd George, he had been unimpressive and Lloyd George had dismissed him for incompetence – thus ensuring that there was little warmth between them thereafter. Law had made him Postmaster-General, and his new appointment in Baldwin's government marked his rise to prominent ministerial office.

Thus began a partnership which was to prove a fruitful one, for although the two men were very different in character they each had qualities which complemented the other. Whereas Baldwin was friendly, approachable and persuasive, shrewd in his judgements of men and situations, Chamberlain was a much more energetic politician, with great application, practical gifts of administration and a command of detail. However, he lacked Baldwin's humanity and his brother's public charm, and Austen noted that 'Neville's manner freezes people'; another contemporary observed that he was 'glacial rather than genial'. There was wide agreement about his ability and dedication, but few regarded him with any affection; his opponents had too often been on the receiving end of what appeared to be his sneering contempt. Baldwin recognised his qualities, and felt that his incisive mind and his independence would make him a strong departmental minister.

Otherwise, the Cabinet remained largely the one Baldwin inherited from his predecessor, and he soon began to wish for a team which was more of a personal creation. However, he was not sure that his position was as yet strong enough for him to wield the prime ministerial axe, and so he felt inhibited from making significant changes.

Mowat has taken a harsh view of Baldwin's Cabinet-making, remarking that he 'badly muffed the opportunity to bring about a reconciliation between his supporters . . . and Austen Chamberlain and his friends'. But Baldwin knew better, for one of his skills was a facility for timing his interventions to bring about the result he wanted. At this time, the mood was not ripe, for several members of the parliamentary party and the Cabinet still felt hostile to the Coalition Conservatives, and may have resigned if Baldwin had attempted to include any of them. In particular, the behaviour of Birkenhead and Horne since 1922 had inspired their distrust, and the thought that such senior figures might be allowed to return to the fold and assume leading positions in the new government was too much for them to bear.

His Cabinet formed, Baldwin soon became unhappy with one of his appointments. Initially pleased that Curzon had agreed to serve under him as Foreign Secretary, he came to doubt his loyalty and his willingness to act in concert with a group of colleagues. Curzon had misgivings about Baldwin as he had had about Lloyd George and Law, under both of whom he had served. But whereas he had confided his opinions about Lloyd George to his wife, he had no such inhibitions about telling Baldwin of his anxieties to his face:

> I am almost in despair as to the way in which foreign policy is carried on in this Cabinet. Any member may make any suggestion . . . the discussion wanders off into hopeless irrelevancies . . . No decision is arrived at and no policy prepared . . . we must act together and the PM must see his FS through.

A POOR INHERITANCE

On assuming the burden of office, Baldwin was confronted with a number of difficult issues. Abroad, the French had occupied the Ruhr coalfield, in protest against the failure of the Germans to pay the post-war reparations which had been laid down in 1921 in settlement of the damage incurred by the allies in the First World War. Until this issue was settled, the prospects for European recovery appeared slender.

At home, there were everywhere signs of economic gloom. Industrial unrest was one symptom of the discontent which many workers felt about their living and working conditions. Unemployment was another. It scarcely fell below ten per cent in the inter-war years, and was linked to the relative, and in some cases, absolute decline of Britain's traditional heavy industries – coal, iron and steel, and shipbuilding. In 1923, exports were already beginning to decline, a downward trend that was to continue for well over a decade.

Few measures of any substance emerged from the legislative programme for 1923, though Neville Chamberlain was responsible for a Housing Act which encouraged the building of private and local authority dwellings. A subsidy of six million pounds per year for 20 years was given for houses for sale, provided they fell within certain restricted categories. It was not a generous measure, but it indicated that Conservatives accepted state responsibility for housing and that local authorities had a role in meeting the need.

Critics were more concerned to point out the limitations of the Act. Labour felt that it favoured private enterprise over public provision, and mainly benefited the lower middle classes rather than those most in need. The passing of the Bill was controversial, and much of the indignation was due to its author. Neville Chamberlain's personality served to antagonise those on the opposition benches, for he contrived to seem bleak and mean, even when he was being constructive.

BALDWIN AND PROTECTION

Baldwin's antipathy to Lloyd George had not relented and in the autumn of 1923 he was worried by thoughts of what trouble the 'dynamic force' might be about to create for him. He was also troubled by th persistent difficulty which beset British governments between the wars – unemployment. The two threats were linked in his mind.

Baldwin could see only one answer to the economic problem, and this was tariff reform. Such a policy, involving imperial preference and duties on food and other goods from outside the Empire, had been urged on the Conservative Party by Joseph Chamberlain in 1903. It was a disruptive and divisive issue then and had damaged the Unionists seriously in the election of 1906.

From the moment Baldwin first entered the House he had been a tariff reformer, as were most Conservatives in the 1906 Parliament. His views were modified by his experiences at the Board of Trade which tended to favour an open trading policy, but in 1923 he saw protection as the only way of dealing with unemployment. Tariffs against countries from outside the Empire would protect home industries and such a boost would enable them to prosper and take on extra workers. He was not immediately contemplating taxes on imported food which would have been too much for many Conservatives to stomach – let alone the alarm which they would have created in the nation at large.

Tariffs had other attractions for Baldwin. The Coalitionists, personally still close to Lloyd George, were also keen on protection. It had been the cause closest to Joseph Chamberlain's heart in his last campaign, and his son Austen was a true believer. Others held a similar attitude, and as long as adopting tariff reform could be done without upsetting the free traders within the party, then there was a good chance of restoring unity. At the same time, the Conservatives would have a distinctive policy which would clearly separate them from their opponents: socialism separated them from Labour, tariff reform would further separate them from Labour, but also from the Liberals – and in particular from Lloyd George.

Reactions to Protection

Talk of tariffs was in the air when Commonwealth leaders met in October 1923 in London for the Imperial Economic Conference. They were interested in some scheme of imperial preference. Baldwin felt it was timely to gauge reactions among Conservatives to such an idea. His Cabinet were aware of the drift of his thinking, and there was some opposition from free trade Conservatives such as Lord Robert Cecil. But it was agreed that when Baldwin addressed the party conference at

Plymouth in October 1923, he should outline his current thinking whilst not committing ministers in general to his ideas or to an early election. His speech included the following extracts, which show that he abided by the Cabinet decision:

> The Government will proceed in the Autumn session to take whatever legislative steps may be necessary in connection with any of the measures to help unemployment which they have proposed. The Board of Trade has been investigating certain distressed industries, and if the case is made out that, on account of the grave unemployment and the nature of the competition to which they are subjected, special help is needed, I shall have no hesitation in asking my friend the Chancellor of the Exchequer to do what he can to safeguard those industries. Mr Bonar Law's pledge, given a year ago, was that there should be no fundamental change in the fiscal arrangements of the country . . . That pledge binds me, and in this Parliament there will be no fundamental change, and I take these words strictly. I am not a man to play with a pledge . . .

Then, rising to his peroration, he continued amidst much cheering: 'To me, at least, the unemployment problem is the most critical problem of our country. I can fight it. I am willing to fight it. I cannot fight it without weapons . . . I have come to the conclusion myself that the only way of fighting this subject is by protecting the home market . . .'

There was no mention in the speech of putting the issue to the country in an early election, and neither is there any evidence that Baldwin was thinking of holding one in the coming parliamentary session. His proposals in the King's Speech implied a year's work. This would provide him with an interval in which he could educate elements of his own party and the country at large in the merits of the protectionist case.

Bonar Law had pledged the party not to act on protection, and Baldwin as Chancellor had agreed not to campaign for its introduction. He felt obliged to honour the commitment, and made it clear in an overflow conference meeting after the main address that he was not contemplating an election. As he told the local agent: 'You may say on my authority that there will be no election.' But Neville Chamberlain and some other leading Conservatives were more doubtful, and favoured an early appeal to the electorate. Chamberlain addressed the same meeting and presented a different picture: 'If we are to deal adequately with the situation of unemployment next winter, then it will be necessary that we should ask to be released from that pledge.'

Some selective protection might have been introduced without putting the issue to the country, but if it was to be extended more generally to cover tariffs on imported food from outside the Empire (as the Dominion leaders wished), then, according to the pledge given, this was something which would require the new policy to be put before the electorate. However, once Baldwin had publicly stated his position, events acquired an unforeseen momentum.

Many Conservatives agreed that protection was desirable, for if limitations were placed on foreign goods coming into Britain, then in theory there was an enlarged home market in which manufacturers could hope to sell their wares. However, the party had not been prepared for a sudden change of policy. Conservative free-traders were alarmed and many who might accept the case for a revision of policy needed assurance that the leadership had carefully prepared the ground so that it could be sold to the nation at large. As Austen Chamberlain remarked after the Plymouth speech, Baldwin had 'said enough to arouse all our opponents to their fullest activity. He has not yet said enough to give guidance to his friends and to rally their enthusiasm in his support.'

Austen Chamberlain urged that there should be clear leadership, saying: 'Let us fight the issue which he has raised on the broadest and most direct lines', by which he was implying the need for an election. Baldwin did not immediately commit himself, and sought to bring Chamberlain into his government. Chamberlain made it clear that this could not be done unless Birkenhead was similarly invited, something which Baldwin knew would be resisted by the rank and file at Westminster.

THE 1923 ELECTION

The Plymouth speech had unleashed powerful forces, and the logic of the argument that protection was needed in the fight against unemployment did seem to be that it was better introduced sooner than later. If there was to be a radical innovation in policy which required an election, why not hold one soon? Baldwin decided that it was time to do so, and on 12 November he asked the King for a dissolution; a general election was to be held later that month. It was a risky strategy. Indeed, an election was not strictly necessary for the government could have continued until 1927, given its comfortable majority.

Some Cabinet colleagues, Curzon among them, were most uneasy. He observed that the Cabinet were 'profoundly shocked and incensed at the way in which they have been treated, and at the recklessness with which the Government and the country entirely contrary to the will and wish of either, have been plunged into a General Election by the arbitrary fiat of one weak and ignorant man'.

Baldwin may have done much to unite the Conservatives by embarking upon protection. Indeed, he showed considerable skill as a party manager in seeking to reconcile the divergent personalities involved, and succeeded in appeasing several on the Coalitionist side. Birkenhead and Austen Chamberlain were willing to campaign for the party from their position outside the government. However, the new policy served also to unite the Liberals, just as it had done in 1903–5. The supporters of Asquith and Lloyd George sank their differences, and agreed on a joint campaign with Liberal candidates chosen from a common slate. With Labour also opposed to protection, Baldwin had a fight on his hands if he was to persuade a reluctant public.

Baldwin's Motives

Some MPs on the opposition benches suspected that Baldwin was acting with calculated guile when he called the snap election. One grouping conjectured that he was deliberately heading for a defeat so that a brief Labour government would take over, find itself in difficulties and lose office to a resurgent Conservative Party. Some subsequent writers have taken the view that he was prepared for defeat, altruistically allowing for a Labour return so that the inexperienced party would have a chance to establish itself as a moderate constitutional party of government. Others have wondered if he was seeking to exclude Labour from a leading place in the two-party system, by allowing the Liberals to recover from their ailing fortunes and re-establish themselves by achieving a good result.

Such theories are highly improbable. Prime ministers like to be on the winning side, and don't normally plan on the assumption that favourable consequences will flow from their defeat. They offer their policies believing, or claiming to believe, that they represent the best course for the country to follow. Baldwin hoped and expected to win, and thought he could do so on a policy of protection which he believed was in the country's interest.

This was Baldwin's initial explanation for his change of mind, but his statements, particularly those made in retrospect, were rather different. In 1925, he placed the emphasis on his desire to reunite the Conservatives. In 1935, he suggested another motive in a conversation with Tom Jones, and this was to pre-empt his arch-rival, Lloyd George. As so often, the Liberal was a central figure in Baldwin's calculations. At that time he was on a tour of the United States, and was thought to be looking for some new programme with which he could hope to rebuild his reputation and recover his national standing. A Liberal initiative involving a call for protection might win over those Coalition Conservatives who were in the political wilderness, along with the possible backing of the press lords, Rothermere and perhaps even Beaverbrook. So Baldwin saw a need for urgency. In his words:

> The Goat was in America. He was on the water when I made the speech, and the Liberals did not know what to say. I had information he was going protectionist and I had to get in quick . . . Dished the Goat, as otherwise he would have got the Party with Austen and FE [Birkenhead], and there would have been an end to the Tory Party as we know it.

This was still not Baldwin's final explanation for his decision to announce his conversion to tariff reform and call an election. He told Jones on another occasion (1943) that he had 'thought it all out by myself . . . I wanted it because I saw no other weapon then to use in the fight against unemployment'. This was more in line with his public utterances at the time.

Quite why he went ahead with his plan can never be precisely assessed. Talk of protectionism as a counter to unemployment was not unknown in Cabinet discussions before October 1923, and Baldwin's adoption of it cannot be regarded as a sudden new departure. He had convinced himself that protection was necessary after long reflection, he was keen to keep Lloyd George from power and it was a means of reuniting the party by enabling the leading Coalitionists to return to the fold. Probably the early election was never intended, but as Anthony Seddon has concluded in *The Conservative Century*, 'events ran out of control' once he had made his Plymouth announcement.

Whatever the reason for Baldwin's decision, it was (in electoral terms) certainly an unwise one. The verdict of Philip Snowden (a future Labour Chancellor of the Exchequer) on Baldwin's chosen policy was harsh but difficult to challenge: 'Suicide during a temporary fit of insanity.' Many have portrayed his actions as indicative of a bout of lunacy, for tariff reform had harmed the party once and was a policy which never brought the Conservatives any reward at the polls.

The election of 1923 was the only one fought primarily on the issue of protection. In different areas of the country, candidates tried to show how it would benefit or damage their particular region and its industries. Labour and the Liberals were in favour of the status quo – free trade. They concentrated on demonstrating that tariffs would increase the cost of living and questioned the likelihood of fuller employment which Conservatives promoted. Their message won the day, and when the results came in it was apparent that the swing against the government was particularly strong in traditional free trade areas such as Lancashire.

Election Results

No party emerged with an absolute majority and although the Conservatives remained the largest party there was no prospect of their continuing in office. They had forfeited 87 seats, and now had 257, as against 191 for Labour and 158 for the Liberals. The message was clear; the argument for protection had been lost. In these circumstances Baldwin agreed that if he was defeated in the House it should be one of the free trade parties which took over. Otherwise, he could have contemplated an alliance with the Liberals to keep Labour out of office. But, he recognised that Labour had earnt a right to show that it could govern. If any manoeuvre by the anti-socialist elements had been devised it might have served to encourage those within the Labour Party who were suspicious of the parliamentary route to socialism.

Baldwin did not resign immediately the results became known. As the outcome had been confused, he was entitled to stay on to meet the new House and challenge his opponents to defeat him. When he met Parliament on 21 January 1924, the Conservatives lost a vote of confidence put down by Labour and backed by the Liberals by 72 votes. He became the first prime minister in the twentieth century to wind up a debate in the certain knowledge that he was about to be defeated. He was, and he resigned. The way was open for Labour to take over the responsibility of office the following day, with Ramsay MacDonald at 10 Downing Street.

Baldwin had anticipated victory in the general election, and his failure to secure it was to have a major impact upon his future behaviour. No more would he be so precipitate. He would allow more time to educate his supporters, and he was to do this on Red Friday in 1925, and over India and rearmament. From a single campaign error, he had drawn a conclusion that was to profoundly influence his conduct in later life. The groundwork before any further innovation must be carefully prepared, and he would tune in carefully to the public mood.

BALDWIN'S SURVIVAL

Most Conservatives were appalled by the prospect of Labour in power, and some would have liked to see Baldwin's leadership at an end as he had allowed this to happen – in their eyes, he had led the party to unnecessary defeat. The short outburst of hostility towards him broke out almost immediately, in part the natural reaction of a party in defeat which had lost its way in the last few years. It had failed to establish a clear identity, even before it joined the Coalition, and after the fall of Lloyd George, its effectiveness was seriously impeded by internal division and the loss of some of its key spokesmen.

Baldwin became a scapegoat, the attack on his leadership coming from the right wing and from the popular press. Newspaper comment in pro-Conservative papers had been adverse even before the election. Indeed, some proprietors opposed the choice of Baldwin in the first place. After his defeat, the sniping continued but the editorial abuse soon died down. Cartoonists exploited several opportunities to portray his condition in defeat, but there was little malice in much of their work.

Some of the criticisms of the newspaper proprietors found an echo in the comments of people within the parliamentary party. There was underlying unease about the direction in which Baldwin wished to take the party, but the way in which protection had been taken up and the election called provided the basis of the assault. Critics seemed to cast doubt on his judgement, which from a Conservative point of view had become even more suspect when he 'let Labour in', in January 1924.

There was also what Middlemas and Barnes have called 'an attempt to bundle Baldwin out of the leadership' by plotters on the right wing. This was planned before Baldwin met parliament, but it had come to nothing. It was based on the idea of an anti-socialist alliance between Conservatives and Liberals to keep Labour out.

For Baldwin this would have been a dishonourable course, for he believed that Labour, recognised by the Speaker as the Chief Opposition Party in 1922, had a right to assume office, and that MacDonald's good sense and moderation would ensure that a Labour government would be less threatening than right-wing Conservatives feared. When the new government took over, the talk of a plot rapidly diminished, and other than receiving sporadic criticism from Curzon Baldwin faced little further internal difficulty. Another election was likely in the not-too-distant future and a leadership challenge might have proved an awkward and untimely decision. Besides, no one could agree on who might succeed him. Austen Chamberlain, the only likely contender, was still identified in Conservative minds as the man who had hoped to fuse his party with the Liberals, and he therefore lacked credibility. So, in the absence of a clear rival, Baldwin retained his position, and Conservatives began to concentrate more on how they might sell his virtues to the electorate: 'If nothing else, the party managers might calculate that he had a reputation as the most honest man in recent politics, who had lost an election rather than break his word.'

Baldwin himself quickly drew the conclusion that he must shelve his tariff policy, for once again protection had proved to be a serious electoral liability. In February, he told Conservatives 'I do not feel justified in advising the party again to submit the proposal for a general tariff to the country, except on the clear evidence that on this matter public opinion is disposed to reconsider its judgement'. Protection ceased to be party policy. However, his pursuit of the cause had enabled Baldwin to reunite the main elements of the party, and, having resolved this issue, he was able to invite the Coalitionists into his Shadow Cabinet. The reconciliation was swiftly carried out, and at a dinner arranged by Neville Chamberlain, his brother and the leader formally made their peace. Birkenhead agreed to rejoin the Front Bench team, and Winston

Churchill was also journeying back towards the party, via a period as a strongly anti-socialist Constitutionalist.

CHANGING THE CONSERVATIVE IMAGE

As tends to happen after such a defeat, it was tempting for many prominent figures in the hierarchy to attribute their lack of success to poor organisation and a failure to get the message across. Certainly, Conservatives from Lancashire and the north-west had a fair point when they accused party headquarters of being out of touch with opinion in the country, and urged that in future there should be greater consultation before policy initiatives were taken up. Baldwin was sensitive to the criticism, and the reforms he carried out were designed to ensure that there was better communication within the party.

He was concerned to prevent Conservatives from relapsing into the sort of negativism they had displayed following defeat in 1906, and was intent on making the party rethink its attitudes. He wished to present a more constructive and forward-looking variety of Conservatism, which would retain the best aspects of the past but present a more humane and appealing front. He wanted to appeal to popular idealism, recognising that there was little chance of securing 'the support of the majority of the nation . . . unless your appeal is not only to their head but to their heart'. In a series of speeches in May and June, he restated his view of Conservatism in a way which was designed to arouse wider support for the party. Social policy was one of his chosen themes, and addressing the Junior Imperial League he promised a long-term strategy for the social services. He believed that 'There has been . . . too much hand-to-mouth legislation, trying to meet acknowledged evils without sufficient foresight and coordination, and with the result that much of the legislation has had to be altered, some hardship relieved and fresh hardships created.' Other new policies involved proposed legislation on insurance, rural and urban housing, and factories; there was also to be a new emphasis upon industrial cooperation. Baldwin was trying to ensure that the party showed that it had a social conscience, and was addressing issues relevant to the daily lives of ordinary people.

In June 1924, a manifesto was published, 'Aims and Principles', and this incorporated much of the thinking set out in Baldwin's earlier *a note on . . .*

CONSERVATISM AND ITS APPEAL IN THE INTERWAR YEARS

The Conservative Party has a record of electoral success in parliamentary systems of government that is unrivalled. Between the wars it held office for more than eighteen years either solely or in a Coalition Government. Two general factors account for their success in this era:

- They benefited from divisions on the Left – the opposition vote was split between the disintegrating Liberal Party and the emergent Labour Party
- The Conservatives were able to adapt and appeal to all classes and groups. (Moderate leaders such as Baldwin appreciated the importance of maintaining a broad appeal)

Other specific factors assisted the Conservative Party:

- A redistribution of constituency boundaries in favour of the Conservative-inclined Home Counties and away from past Liberal strongholds
- The workings of the 'first past the post' electoral system in a three-party situation
- The loss to the opposition of some 80 Irish Nationalist MPs from the House of Commons (removed by the Irish settlement of 1920–22)
- The enfranchisement of women may have benefited the Conservatives

The social base of the Conservative Party had expanded, and it won an increasing amount of support from the business and commercial community. After the 1914–18 war, the Conservatives in the House of Commons had a strong business element.

The appeal of the Conservative Party also broadened as it attracted the vote of the middle-class artisan inhabitants of the new suburbs and many members of the working class who were swayed by deference and the belief that the Conservatives were the 'natural party of government'. This broad appeal enabled the Conservatives to portray their party as one that transcended class divisions; they were 'a truly national party', whereas their opponents represented 'sectional interests'.

---

speeches. The sterile era of Bonar Law was to be a thing of the past, and after 1924 Conservatism moved into a new phase in which policy moved to the left and a new note of collectivism emerged, by which the need for a greater degree of state involvement in and regulation of economic life was embraced. This was to be an important characteristic of the Baldwin era and indeed of future Conservatism. Above all, however,

Baldwin's 'New Conservatism' stressed the need for a social policy, an element which had been shelved during the negative period earlier in the century. Individual Conservatives, including Baldwin himself, had never been averse to policies of social betterment, and along with F. E. Smith (later Lord Birkenhead) he had supported them before the war and under the Lloyd George Coalition. There was much to be done in housing, education and industrial relations, and neither negative reaction nor protection had aroused the enthusiasm of the voters. Now was the time to advance a new reforming creed.

RESPONDING TO THE LABOUR GOVERNMENT

MacDonald's short-lived minority government was unable to achieve a great deal, for it was dependent on the Liberals and felt the need to demonstrate its sense of moderation and responsibility. Apart from the success of Wheatley's Housing Act which boldly developed and recast Chamberlain's earlier measure, there was little domestic achievement to its credit. Financial policies under Philip Snowden at the Exchequer were notably orthodox, and the government disappointed its critics by cutting expenditure and taxes. Such elements of protection as already existed were removed; the McKenna Duties which had been introduced in wartime by the Asquith Coalition to impose tariffs on the importation of certain luxury goods were abandoned. Free trade Liberals could feel at ease with Snowden's performance at the Treasury.

By his own admission, Baldwin was not a particularly effective Leader of the Opposition, for he lacked the partisanship which could have cruelly exploited the government's weakness. He personally liked the new Prime Minister, and had some sympathy for his ministers in their predicament as they tried to come to terms with the realities of power. One journalist portrayed him as 'simply the chief patient in the Tory convalescent home, knocking the dust off his favourite books and soliloquising over the greatness he has lost'. Many Conservatives would have liked to see a more vigorous performance; they wanted to see ministers harried for their mistakes. But Baldwin knew that much of the legislation being introduced had already been in the pipeline when he left office, and it was difficult to attack estimates and policies with which the Conservatives had once been associated.

Neville Chamberlain, the author of much of the new 'Aims and Principles' document, was keen to see the party embrace new ideas and launch new policies. Baldwin was less committal on the details of policies, for he knew that he was open to the charge that if initiatives were especially necessary, he should have done more to introduce them the previous year. But what he did do was to set the tone for Conservatism in the future in his speeches, ensuring that the party was presented as an effective alternative government, ready and prepared to take over as soon as the opportunity arose. He managed to keep the party in the forefront of political discourse, while he awaited the expected fall of the government.

The Labour ministry came to grief over its relations with Communism at home and abroad. In September, Baldwin and Asquith were able to exploit the government's embarrassment over relations with Russia. MacDonald had given de facto recognition to the Bolshevik government, and had negotiated a commercial agreement. Two treaties were to be signed offering the Russians 'most-favoured nation status' and loan facilities, and they were to be ratified by Parliament in the autumn. But the issue of the treaties was suddenly dwarfed by another question, the government's handling of the Campbell case.

J. R. Campbell, the editor of the *Worker's Weekly*, had been charged in the courts with inciting the troops to mutiny. However, during the summer recess the Attorney-General withdrew the prosecution, arguing that to go ahead would be a gift to the Communist propaganda machine for Campbell had had a distinguished war record. The Conservatives contended that the withdrawal was a purely political move. Baldwin tabled a motion of censure, though he was content for the issue to go before a Select Committee of the House of Commons. Outside the House he preferred to concentrate his attack on the treaties rather than the merits of the withdrawn prosecution.

The government decided to make the motion of censure an issue of confidence, and it was heavily defeated by 364 votes to 198. MacDonald resigned and a new general election was arranged. The campaign was a short one, and Baldwin used it to portray Labour ministers as being in the hands of 'those extremist forces which appear to control it'. He also pointed to the failure of any imaginative scheme to tackle unemployment, noting that repealing the McKenna Duties had served to make the problem worse.

In the campaign Baldwin was skilful in his use of the opportunity to broadcast on radio. MacDonald's was recorded at a live meeting, and sounded as though he was 'a hectoring demagogue' (Middlemas and Barnes), whereas Baldwin showed himself to be a master of the new medium. Recorded in the Director-General's private office, he appeared to be quietly in control, speaking intimately to people in their homes. He caught the public mood as he urged the need for 'a sane commonsense Government, not carried away by revolutionary theories or harebrained schemes . . . we cannot afford the luxury of academic Socialists or revolutionary agitation'. Moderate that he was, he could play the anti-Bolshevik theme as well as his more partisan supporters; as he announced, 'no gospel founded on hate will ever be the gospel of our people'.

Polling day was 29 October, and four days before this the *Daily Mail* published a letter reputed to be from the Russian Communist leader Zinoviev, President of the Comintern, to the Communist Party in Britain, containing instructions for the preparation of armed rebellion. This letter might have been dismissed as an obvious forgery and an election stunt, but it was made to appear serious and genuine by the publication by the Foreign Office of a letter to the Soviet chargé d'affairs, protesting against such propaganda and interference in British domestic affairs.

This was the culmination of a campaign in which the Red Scare had featured strongly. Posters, cartoons and jingles ran the familiar themes, a contemporary ditty being:

Bolshevik, Bolshevik, where have you been?
Over to ENGLAND where the Reds are still green.

Baldwin exploited this theme and declared that it was time to tell the Russians, 'Hands off England'. He accepted the genuineness of the Zinoviev Letter, even though it has subsequently been demonstrated to have been a forgery in which Central Office was implicated. It probably only served to accentuate the anti-Labour trend which was clearly there anyway, but coming as it did so close to the election its release was a shady manoeuvre designed to discredit Labour as 'soft on Communism', a ploy which worked.

In the election of 1924, Labour representation fell to 152 MPs although its vote continued to advance. The Liberals suffered a serious setback (down from 151 to 40), while the Conservatives gained a massive total of 419 in a House of Commons of 615 members. It was apparent that the Conservative Party was identified by many voters as the safest repository for the anti-socialist vote – they saw in Baldwinian Conservatism the image of social stability and order with which they felt at ease.

timeline	1923	May	Baldwin became Conservative leader and Prime Minister
		October	Plymouth Speech: outlined thinking on protection
		November	Snap election: badly defeated
	1924		Survived as leader, despite criticism
			Improved Conservative image: new manifesto, 'Aims and Principles'
			Put down censure motion on MacDonald government over prosecution of J. R. Campbell
		October	Election victory, four days after publication of Zinoviev Letter

Points to Consider

1) 'Baldwin obtained the leadership of the Conservative Party as much by luck as because of his ability.' Is this a fair comment?
2) Why was Baldwin attracted to a policy of tariff revision?
3) Why did he call an election in December 1923? Was it a necessary one?
4) In what ways did he refashion the Conservative Party in the period of opposition to the first Labour government?

THE SECOND ADMINISTRATION, 1924–9

In the circumstances in which the election was held, the triumph of the Conservatives in October 1924 was a foregone conclusion. It was a massive victory. Their popular vote was up by nearly two and a half million, only in part a reflection of fielding more candidates. More important was the fact that those Conservatives won a larger proportion of the vote; the average share rose from 42.6 per cent to 51.9 per cent. Overall, they gained the backing of 48.3 per cent of the electorate, and this was the nearest the party had been to an overall majority for 50 years.

The murmurs of criticism against Baldwin's leadership subsided for this time he had led them to a conclusive victory. The result was a triumph for his moderate approach, and for those who wanted to cast an anti-Labour vote the Baldwinian Conservative Party provided a safe haven – standing as it did for stability and order. The Liberal Party was no longer a realistic contender for power, and with MacDonald and Baldwin facing each other across the House there was unlikely to be fundamental disagreement over policy or personal vitriol between the two front benches. Party strife was to be at a low ebb.

FORMING A CABINET

Baldwin was in a strong position, though even he did not claim that the success was a purely personal one: 'I am under no temptation to believe that the victory was the result of leadership.' Armed with an overwhelming majority in the House, he could assume that he had a whole five-year term ahead. He was able to create a Cabinet of his own choosing and this time he had a freer hand than in 1923. Those Conservatives who had previously wanted to continue with the Coalition were now willing to be reconciled. Their only alternative was to remain outside in the cold. The Carlton Club meeting was put behind the party, and with the greater ability now available, Baldwin was able to construct a talented front bench.

Of the former Coalitionists, Birkenhead became Secretary of State for India and Austen Chamberlain took over the Foreign Office. Balfour – a strong opponent of Baldwin in October 1922 – was not initially in the Cabinet, but replaced Curzon as Lord Chancellor (Curzon, disappointed not to be given his former position as Foreign Secretary, died in 1925). Austen's half-brother, Neville, who had served in the 1923 government, became Minister of Health (a portfolio which then also covered Housing and Local Government) and was to prove one of the most able figures in the Cabinet.

The big surprise, however, was the appointment of Winston Churchill to the Exchequer, for he had little understanding of economic theory and neither had he expressed any interest in it. At the time, he was not even a Conservative. He had left Balfour's government in 1903, been a prominent Liberal and colleague of Lloyd George and stood at a by-election earlier in 1924 as an 'anti-socialist Constitutionalist'. Unopposed, he was now returned as a Constitutionalist, but was yet to rejoin the Conservative Party – though he finally became a member of the Carlton Club in 1925 and thereby re-established his true-blue credentials.

It is said that on being offered the Chancellorship, Churchill thought he was being offered the position of Chancellor of the Duchy of Lancaster. However, although his personal suitability was in doubt, as was his ability to work with the Treasury advisers ('if they were soldiers or generals, I would understand what they were talking about'), the choice of such an acknowledged and passionate free trader had the merit of illustrating Baldwin's determination to shun protectionism which had so damaged his cause a year earlier. Besides, a loose cannon such as Churchill was safer in the Cabinet than on the back benches, where he might have been a focus for trouble, for he was a person of formidable abilities and strong opinions.

With the Coalitionists now safely contained, Baldwin could feel secure. His old enemy, Lloyd George, was clearly isolated. However, an obsession with the activities of the charismatic Liberal remained a guiding theme in Baldwin's thinking, long after the Welshman had fallen from power.

BALDWIN'S PRIORITIES

The new government was concerned to promote national unity, and its programme was to involve measures of social amelioration and an effort to cope with the endemic unemployment which previous governments had been unable to solve. Not all of Baldwin's colleagues shared his priorities, and it was necessary to restrain those for whom a negative anti-socialism was at the core of their thinking. Some of them wanted to clamp down on the activities of trade unions and were doubtful of the loyalty and patriotism of their leaders. Baldwin was more sympathetic to the Labour movement and wanted to encourage its political wing to maintain its commitment to the democratic process. He had a distaste for those businessmen who were willing to deny justice to their workers in the pursuit of profit.

Although his protectionist theme had been quietly abandoned, Baldwin had something distinctive to offer – an interest in moderate social reform. Baldwin was cast in a Disraelian mould. He warmed to the rhetoric of 'one nation', and had a similar interest in national unity. Britain in the 1920s was a land of 'two nations', and Baldwin saw the need for Conservatism to address this division if the social fabric was to be maintained; social harmony was the key to political stability. In this spirit, he worked with his energetic Minister of Health, Chamberlain, to tackle issues such as the Poor Law, health insurance, unemployment insurance and insurance against sickness and old age; they linked together in what Middlemas and Barnes describe as 'the circle of security for the worker'.

THE RETURN TO THE GOLD STANDARD

The post-war Conservatives favoured an orthodox financial policy, based upon the idea of a balanced budget and a return to the Gold Standard at its pre-war parity. Soon after Baldwin returned to Number 10 Downing Street, the issue of a 'return to gold' came to the fore. The Gold Standard had been temporarily suspended in 1919, and over the following years the value of the pound sterling against the dollar fluctuated considerably, at lower levels than it had previously been fixed (£1 = $4.86). In 1925, the Gold (Export) Act was due to lapse, and it was necessary to decide whether to go back to the Gold Standard or to introduce alternative legislation.

There was little dispute among financiers, for the overwhelming weight of City opinion wanted a return to gold at the pre-war parity. The Governor of the Bank of England was in favour, and so was the Treasury. They all looked back to the days when the pound sterling commanded the respect of the world, and felt that 'being back on gold' would restore London to its place of leadership and help promote European monetary stability – for Britain had a reputation as an experienced financial centre.

Critics of the Gold Standard were fearful of the effect on exports, for at the pre-war rate the pound would be overvalued in relation to other currencies; this would make exports over-priced. If industrialists were to keep their goods competitive in the export markets, they would need to cut costs and this would involve cuts in wages, particularly in the heavy industries which relied on selling abroad. Mining was the obvious example, and some economists saw the likely outcome.

John Maynard Keynes was one of the few contemporary voices raised against the idea of returning to the Gold Standard, and his views were later published as *The Economic Consequences of Mr Churchill*:

> [Mr Churchill] was just asking for trouble. For he was committing himself to force down money-wages and all money values, without any idea how it was done . . . [the result] must be war, until those who are economically weakest are beaten to the ground.

As Chancellor, Churchill listened to his arguments and wanted to hear the views of anyone who had an opinion on the matter. He lacked a technical grasp of the issue himself, and recognised the need to consult widely. As the overwhelming weight of advice was on the side of the Governor of the Bank of England, he went with the majority; indeed, he would have been a brave Chancellor to have done otherwise, given his known lack of expertise. Once Churchill had formed an opinion, Baldwin backed his judgement and defended it in the Cabinet and outside.

In retrospect, the 'return to gold' (especially at the pre-war level) was seen as an error, and Churchill himself later came to regret it. Damage was done to British exports, and manufacturers, particularly the coal-owners, did make wage-cuts and seek to reduce employment as a way of containing their costs of production.

THE ECONOMIC SITUATION: UNEMPLOYMENT

The persistent domestic problem which confronted British governments between the wars was unemployment. Although some economists and businessmen were prepared to contemplate bold solutions, most politicians despaired of finding an answer and awaited an economic upturn. Baldwin's government was no more original or successful than MacDonald's, and the number of unemployed was marginally worse in 1929 when he left office than when he had assumed the premiership. In 1924 the figure was 1,229,000; in 1929 it had risen to 1,344,000.

The basic problem concerned the decay of old, traditional industries such as coal, iron and steel, shipbuilding and cotton. The signs of decline had been evident since the late nineteenth century, but the First World War had brought a temporary halt to the long-term downward trend. War had given a boost to Britain's industrial performance, but so also it had encouraged other countries to develop their own resources. When the war ended, Britain's familiar export markets no longer offered the same possibilities. The massive increase in US and Japanese shipping during the war meant that there were too many ships in existence after 1918; the shipbuilders' market dried up. The world-wide expansion of coal production led to a glut of a commodity the demand for which was anyway shrinking – oil replaced coal for much of the world's shipping, and the development of gas and electricity lowered demand still further.

Much of British industry was still using out-of-date equipment, and obsolescent plant and machines led to high costs and low productivity. Fallen demand for often expensive exports encouraged the growth of depressed areas which were characterised by persistent levels of high unemployment. Not all the country was affected, and the workers were concentrated in those regions that had been industrial leaders several decades earlier, particularly Durham, Lancashire, Staffordshire, Yorkshire, Scotland and South Wales. Even in the depressed areas, the picture was not universal, and often particular towns had branches of industry which suffered most. These ailing industries were not replaced by new ones for the expanding light engineering works of inter-war Britain were often located elsewhere, in the Midlands and south.

Baldwin's personal mission was industrial peace between employer and employee. He had much less to offer the unemployed, and had little insight into the means of bringing about economic recovery. One action, the return to the Gold Standard, had aggravated the situation. One possible solution, tariff reform, was ruled out. It was, in the eyes of ministers, a matter of awaiting a recovery in exports. Improved trading conditions in America, associated with the boom of 1927–8, were of temporary assistance, and exports did increase in those years.

Businessmen and the unemployed were only too aware of the problems in the affected areas, but in large parts of the country the situation was much better. For many people, the standard of living improved and the reasonably well off were able to enjoy the first fruits of the mass market which was catering for leisure needs. It was easy for people in the more Conservative south not to appreciate the despair of the decaying regions, and Baldwin's response to the King's Speech in February 1928 encouraged a belief that things were going well. He pointed out that over a million more people were employed in industry than was the case six or seven years before, and also stated that 'the prosperity and expansion of the "new" trades – motor car manufactures, artificial silk, gramophones – [was] going far to absorb the displacement of labour from some of the depressed "heavy industries"'.

Baldwin was most effective in defence of his government, but his response did not answer the fears of many who lived in the depressed areas and others who discerned the trends of the time. It was true that more people were in employment than before, but it was becoming very clear that the problem of unemployment was not just a residual legacy of the war, but indicated that British industry was ill-adapted to a new commercial era. In particular, despite Baldwin's assertions that labour from some of the decaying areas was being absorbed, the difficulties of those regions were getting steadily worse. By 1928, unemployment in coal, cotton, steel and building was increasing, and the situation was declining most rapidly in the north and in Wales.

In 1927–8, Baldwin still tended to talk in the same language as he had done in 1924. He urged that the staple industries should put their house in order and ensure that they became more competitive by reducing excess capacity. It seemed a harsh analysis, and one which brought little comfort to victims of recession. However, he was not disposed to contemplate a return to his previous policy of tariff revision, although a number of his colleagues were beginning to wonder whether protection was necessary – especially for the hard-pressed iron and steel industries.

Selective use of import controls would have been possible under the terms of the Safeguarding of Industries Act which, if interpreted generously, would have allowed for quite a wide use of tariffs. Amery and other ministers were keen to see such limitations on imports, and the steel companies were urging Baldwin to concede their case for some protection. But Churchill, whilst prepared to go some way to conciliate his colleagues, would not yield on this. He felt that steel production was an industry so central to the economy, that to have protected it alone would have been unrealistic; steel-users would have expected protection for their components as well. If they paid more for their steel, they would need to be compensated by protection, so that they could charge higher prices in the home market. If the government allowed this, then it would be reneging on Baldwin's election promise. The Prime Minister accepted the force of Churchill's case, and so was forced to deny himself the one weapon which he believed might have been effective.

Failing to grasp the gravity of the underlying economic issues, the government dealt only in palliatives. A committee investigating unemployment relief in 1927 noted that the actual levels of benefit were 'hardly recognisable through the tangled mass of opportunist legislation'. The Unemployment Insurance Act of that year provided unlimited instead of six-month cover to anyone employed for 15 weeks a year. The Derating of Industry Act (1929) relieved businessmen of some three-quarters of their rate burdens, releasing some 27 million pounds for investment in their companies' future prospects. Otherwise, apart from a modest programme of development of public services, ministers did nothing, avoiding, in the words of the party manifesto (1929), 'hasty and ill-considered schemes which could lead to wasteful and unfruitful expenditure'.

INDUSTRIAL RELATIONS

By 1922, it seemed as though the industrial confrontation of post-war Britain was at an end and Baldwin was keen to preserve the new-found harmony. Not all his backbenchers shared his approach and it was a proposal by a Scottish lawyer, Macquisten, for a Bill to cripple the Labour Party financially by changing the rules concerning the trade union political levy, which provoked the Prime Minister to firm resistance.

Along with many Conservatives, Baldwin had reservations about a system which assumed that a member of an affiliated trade union wished to pay the levy, unless he specifically 'contracted out' from so doing. Out of a combination of inertia and lack of knowledge, there were a number of trade unionists who supported Labour finances despite their preference for another party. Baldwin knew of the strength of feeling on the issue, and recognised that Macquisten's initiative would deal an effective blow to the financial connection between the unions and the Labour Party, thus providing an obstacle to Labour's further growth. However, he was less concerned about the threat posed by MacDonald and his supporters, and much more anxious about the possibility of provoking class warfare. Accordingly, the government put down an amendment to the Bill, and it was on this that the Prime Minister made one of his finest speeches in 1925.

Baldwin spoke for an hour to an attentive House and after delivering a homily on industrial relations in the family firm 'where nobody ever got the sack', he turned to the subject of the Private Member's Bill:

> I want my party to make a gesture to the country . . . We have our majority. We believe in the justice of the bill . . . But we are going to withdraw our hand. We are not going to push our political advantage home at a moment like this . . . We at any rate are not going to fire the first shot . . . Although I know there are those who work for different ends from most of us in this House, yet there are many in all ranks and all parties who will re-echo my prayer; 'Give peace in our time, O Lord'.

Not only did his remarks kill the Bill. They provided Baldwin with a new personal ascendancy at Westminster and in the country. In the Cabinet, the parliamentary party and the press, the reaction was congratulatory for this seemed to be the speech of a true leader, endowed with an unusual degree of moral authority. Among Labour MPs, there was also much admiration for the spirit of conciliation.

Of course, expressions of general benevolence and goodwill cost little and for many working people the government was to be judged more by its actions than on the basis of its rhetoric. Within a few months of Baldwin's debating triumph, the reality of life in the coalmining industry was to test the Conservatives' resolve to shun partisanship and pursue the course of industrial peace to the utmost.

After the Conservative success in the 1924 election, some trade unionists felt that they would have to improve their working conditions via industrial militancy, for the political wing of the Labour movement, the Labour Party, was likely to be in opposition for four or five years. Conflict was made more likely following the government's decision to return to the Gold Standard which had weakened the export market for British manufacturers. In the coal industry, miners were once again threatened with wage reductions as the owners tried to protect their profits in adverse economic circumstances. Many other workers sympathised with the miners' plight and feared that the attack on their wages might be but a prelude to a more widespread attempt to keep wages down. Such anxieties were intensified by an alleged remark of Baldwin's (reported in the *Daily Herald*), suggesting that 'all the workers of this country have got to take reductions in wages to help put industry on its feet'.

INDUSTRIAL STRIFE

When the coal owners announced their intention of imposing longer hours and reduced wages, the miners, led by their uncompromising leader, A. J. Cook, were determined to resist. They had the backing of other unions in the TUC. Faced by such a demonstration of unity and the prospect of a general strike, Baldwin stepped back from the brink of civil confrontation. In July 1925, after a few days of frantic consultation of a type not normally associated with Baldwin, he agreed to subsidise the industry until May 1926, as a way of maintaining existing levels of wages and profits. At the same time, on Friday 31 July, he announced the appointment of a Royal Commission into the running of the coal mines. The *Daily Herald* christened that day as 'Red Friday'.

Baldwin had played for time for he recognised that the country was not prepared for industrial dislocation: 'We were not ready', he later observed. Whilst Sir Herbert Samuel's enquiry was being conducted, plans were made to establish a national strike-breaking body, the Organisation for the

Maintenance of Supplies, to recruit and train voluntary workers. Sir John Anderson, an eminent civil servant, was asked to prepare the country to cope with a general strike if and when it came. Meanwhile, twelve leading members of the Communist Party were locked up for they were seen as men likely to exploit any forthcoming industrial conflict.

Some MPs within the Tory Party were sceptical about the policy adopted by the government. Right-wing members found Baldwin's attitude too conciliatory and spoke of capitulation. Within the Cabinet, there was some feeling that the subsidy would only postpone the inevitable confrontation, and that 'loyal' miners might feel affronted by the spectacle of ministers giving in to the threat of forceful persuasion. However, with the strong support of Neville Chamberlain and Churchill, Baldwin got his way and in so postponing a general strike earned himself the plaudits of the King who congratulated him on his 'wisdom and justice' in a 'serious crisis'.

For Chamberlain, news of the subsidy meant that 'a load fell away from my heart'. However, this was not the typical reaction of Conservatives in the country, for party activists felt it was time to deal with the political power of the union. They heard with alarm the language of A. J. Cook who announced in August that he did not 'care a hang for any government . . . We have already beaten not only the employers, but the strongest Government in modern times'. Many felt that the government had been taken unawares and should have been better prepared for the dispute, but Baldwin, who believed in the importance of educating people to the realities of the situation, felt the need to stress that the implications of a general strike had not been fully understood. He told the House of Commons that 'It is a very much easier thing to be rattled into a fight than to be rattled into peace.'

The immediate crisis over, Baldwin sat back and awaited the findings of the Royal Commission. His reputation stood highly at that time, for outside the party it was widely felt that he had acquitted himself well, and he could bask in the agreeable public mood. However, by early spring battle lines were being drawn in advance of publication of the report. *The Times* dwelt on the menace of Communism in the unions, whilst in the Labour movement there was discussion among left-wingers of the damage caused by capitalism.

The Commission reported in March 1926, and its findings were not pleasing to either miners or owners. The report recommended in the

THE SOFT-WORD PUZZLE.

Mr. Baldwin. "CAN ANYBODY THINK OF ANOTHER WORD FOR 'SUBSIDY'?"

In 1926, some members of the Cabinet seek a solution to the 'coal problem'.
Baldwin and Churchill pore over the evidence, Austen and Neville Chamberlain
(and Joynson – Hicks on the right) check reference books, and Birkenhead looks on.

long term a reorganisation of the mines, including the amalgamation of smaller pits, to produce a more modern and viable industry. In the short term, rather than continue a policy of indefinite subsidy, there was no alternative to wage cuts. The owners were unenthusiastic about the long-term recommendations, and were primarily interested in lowering their wage costs. The miners deplored such wage cuts and were unwilling to take assurances of future benefits which would be brought about by reorganisation. They approved of the proposed restructuring, but were concerned with the immediate threat to miners' pay and conditions. Cook spoke for many when he demanded 'Not a penny off the pay, not a minute on the day'.

The TUC discerned greater merit in the recommendations and saw them as a basis for further discussion. Baldwin and the TUC leaders hoped that Cook and his colleagues might accept cuts so that they could then pressure the owners to make concessions as well. But neither the owners nor the workers were willing to back down in spite of Baldwin's reassuring rhetoric, and on 1 May a coal strike began.

THE GENERAL STRIKE, 4–12 MAY 1926

The TUC was still in negotiation with Cabinet ministers, but late on Sunday night (2 May) news came through that the compositors (printers) at the *Daily Mail* were refusing to allow the Monday paper to go to press because they objected to the contents of an editorial condemning strike action. This gave Baldwin a pretext for ending further discussion. He demanded that the TUC should repudiate their action, and call off any plans for a general strike. The TUC could agree to the first requirement, but by the time two TUC spokesmen had returned to Downing Street in the early hours for further discussion of the impasse, Baldwin had retired to bed.

For ministers, who were aware that strike notices had been sent out the day before, the decision of the printers was the last straw in a tense drama. They had been awaiting any sign of a response to the notices, and this was it. In their eyes, the situation was hopeless, and so they broke off negotiations. When Baldwin saw the TUC negotiators to deliver the ultimatum that they must back down, he was speaking for all of his colleagues.

Baldwin broke off discussion at a time when there was still just a glimmer of hope that a strike might be avoided. He had not provoked it, though arguably he could have done more in the last-minute negotiations to fend it off. Mowat (*Britain Between the Wars, 1918–40*) was critical of his behaviour in the final 48 hours of talks and argued that 'in this sense' he was responsible for the strike. Seaman (*Post-Victorian Britain, 1902–51*) has taken a similar view, and claims that Baldwin's cessation of the talks was 'the most provocative action taken by a participant'.

It is true that several members of the TUC were privately very unenthusiastic about the idea of a general strike, and if Baldwin could have divided those people from the leaders of the National Union of Miners there was a possibility of a settlement. But it is doubtful whether this was possible even if there had been more vigorous action by ministers. Baldwin probably concluded that the TUC leaders had no significant chance of holding back the troops until there had been a trial of strength – the more so as the strike notices had already gone out. Some of the union leaders were keen for a confrontation, and there was no chance that the miners would yield. Baldwin had already tried the approach of a subsidy. Another would have been anathema to his party which contained its share of what Baldwin regarded as hard-faced men. There was no chance that the owners would pay increased wages. Both sides, miners and mine owners, were preparing for the seemingly inevitable conflict.

The strike represented a serious defeat for Baldwin's hopes of industrial harmony, and he told the House of Commons on 4 May that:

I have worked for two years to the utmost of my ability in one direction. I have failed so far. Everything that I care for is being smashed to bits at this moment. That does not take away from me either my faith or my courage. We may in this House today be full of strife. Before long the angel of peace, with healing in his wings, will be among us again, and when he comes let us be there to meet him. I shall start again . . .

During the nine days of general action (4–12 May), Baldwin was the man to keep the country calm. He was able to keep his colleagues under control, even Churchill, one of the most staunchly anti-socialist of them all. The Chancellor was placed in the editorship of the *British Gazette*, the official government organ of propaganda, and this gave him an outlet for his forceful views on the unions. For Baldwin the main advantage of the arrangement was to stop Churchill from 'doing worse things' and, as it was, his intemperate attacks on 'militants' and 'Bolsheviks' did little harm other than to his own reputation with many trade unionists who had anyway long viewed him with suspicion. Baldwin declined a suggestion that Churchill should be allowed to take over the BBC as part of the emergency arrangements.

Baldwin himself used the radio effectively and in his broadcast of 8 May his language was characteristically moderate. He struck a balance, arguing for firmness over the constitutional principle and conciliation between the parties to the dispute. He concluded by saying:

> I am a man of peace. I am longing and looking and praying for peace. But I will not surrender the safety and the security of the British Constitution . . . It placed me in power eighteen months ago by the largest majority accorded to any party for many, many years. Have I done anything to forfeit that confidence? Cannot you trust me to ensure a square deal and to ensure even justice between man and man?

On the constitutional issue he was unwavering, for he saw the general strike weapon as abhorrent to the principles of democracy. The threat of general industrial action was a challenge to the constitutional rights and freedom of the nation which must be resisted. He would not capitulate in the face of such intimidation. The coal dispute was a different matter, one that could be solved by peaceful negotiation of which he was in favour. When the General Strike was over, then the miners' situation could be addressed, but not before the wide national stoppage was unconditionally called off. In the meantime, ministers waited 'for the strike to wear itself out'.

The General Strike was skilfully handled and Baldwin seemed imperturbable – on the one hand upholding the supremacy of the state and on the other, keeping things calm and avoiding needless provocation. The government was able to make use of the BBC for spreading its version of events and the public, whilst not unsympathetic to the miners, agreed with the message that the challenge to the Constitution must be resisted.

Whilst the events unfolded, life went on without excessive disturbance. The fine weather helped maintain spirits and good temper. Though there was some sporadic violence, particularly in the mining areas, it was not the general pattern. The government's strike-breaking transport arrangements, though sometimes sabotaged by irate demonstrators, ensured that many people got to work. There was no widespread chaos of the type that more militant trade unionists had expected, and it was not ministers but the TUC negotiators who were forced to climb down. At midday on 12 May, they arrived to see the Prime Minister in what amounted to an unconditional surrender. Baldwin felt able to 'thank God for [the] decision', and over the coming days he used his influence to persuade employers such as those in the railway industry, to adopt a generous and forgiving attitude to those who had gone on strike. This was contrary to the instincts of some employers, but Baldwin's conciliatory approach largely prevailed.

The General Strike was over, but the miners continued their struggle through the summer and the autumn. Both sides, owners and workers, showed much obstinacy in their determination to hold out. At first, Baldwin worked for a settlement, but by July he was becoming impatient with the intransigence displayed by spokesmen on either side. 'Leave it alone, we are so tired', he observed a month later. Neville Chamberlain noted that 'SB has suffered most from the strike; he too is worn out and has no spirit left'. The Prime Minister was on the verge of nervous exhaustion and contrary to the King's wishes he left for a month's holiday in Aix-les-Bains. Churchill was left to handle the negotiations and despite his belligerence in May he now displayed more sympathy for the miners. Both the Chancellor and his leader found the owners unyielding, and Baldwin privately confided his view that they were 'stupid and discourteous'.

By November, the strike was almost over for the miners were being starved back to work. In December, cowed and embittered, they were working an eight-hour day for lower wages than before. There was acute resentment in the mining communities, and as the stoppage had dragged on goodwill towards Baldwin personally began to ebb away. His reputation for fairness and moderation had taken a battering. He was criticised for his lack of energy in pursuing a settlement – moderation without action was not enough.

The King hoped for a peace that would last, but some Conservatives were keen to exploit their victory, and Baldwin, who too easily surrendered to their pressure, acquiesced in their plans. Rather than insist that they did not 'push [the] political advantage home' as he had in 1925, he allowed himself to be persuaded to introduce legislation outlawing sympathetic strikes or those 'designed or calculated to coerce the government'. Other aspects of the Trades Disputes Act of 1927 included a stricter definition of peaceful picketing and a change to the law on payment of the political levy. From now onwards, trade unionists wishing to contribute to the political fund of their union had to 'contract in' if they wished to do so. The measure was a blow to the Labour movement, for party income would inevitably fall by a significant amount.

Baldwin did not like the legislation, and had never wished to penalise the trade unions for their industrial action. However, as Prime Minister he was unwilling to exert leadership and restrain his more partisan colleagues. In so doing, he was accepting the main features of the proposal against which he had so eloquently spoken in 1925. Even then, however, he had recognised that there was a case for 'contracting out', and the events of the last two years could be said to have shown him that some of the unions had not merited the trust he had placed in them. That message was put to him very clearly at the 1926 Conservative Conference, where one speaker 'urged the conference not to be content with pious resolutions . . . we demand as delegates that these laws shall be altered . . . Get on with it or get out'.

LEGISLATIVE ACTION: SOCIAL REFORM

Under Baldwin, the Conservative tradition of 'doing something' about social reform revived. We have seen that the Prime Minister shared the Disraelian belief in 'one nation', and felt that reform was right and just. Moreover, he believed that if governments did not tackle social disharmony then political stability would be undermined. As his mentor had noted, 'the palace is not safe, while the cottage is not happy'. Given Baldwin's opposition to class conflict, paternalistic welfare measures were likely to be on the cards.

The responsibility for implementing this approach fell on the Minister of Health, Neville Chamberlain, who proved to be one of the ablest and most energetic administrators that the Conservative Party have produced in the twentieth century. He saw reform as necessary for the national good as well as for party advantage, and commented that 'unless we leave our mark as social reformers, the country will take it out of us hereafter'. A. J. P. Taylor described him as 'the most effective social reformer of the interwar years', but noted that unfortunately, he 'sounded mean even when he was conferring benefits'.

Chamberlain's manner was in no way helpful, for – seemingly harsh and unsympathetic – he also often expressed himself badly. Moreover, he was unwilling to suffer fools gladly. Whereas Baldwin was emollient and reassuring, his minister was often overbearing and excessively combative, and his opponents found this approach offensive for he often crushed them in debate. The Prime Minister told him on one occasion that he gave the impression in the House of Commons 'of looking upon the Labour Party as dirt'. His response was revealing: 'intellectually, they *are* dirt'.

For all of his personal unattractiveness, Neville Chamberlain was also a man of administrative efficiency with a real commitment to social improvement. He had had long experience of local government, like his father before him, and had acted as Opposition spokesman on housing and health. He had entertained the idea of being Chancellor of the Exchequer but recognised his limitations, and noted that 'I ought to be a great Minister of Health, but am not likely to be more than a second-rate Chancellor'. His new responsibilities also included housing and local government, and as such he was to be responsible for a series of important piecemeal reforms. His concern was more to do with efficient administration than with social justice, but in a whole series of fields – local government reorganisation, reform of the Poor Law, housing and pensions – he left his mark. Blake noted the widespread nature of his contribution and labelled him as 'the equivalent of Sir Richard Cross', a constructive and energetic Home Secretary in Disraeli's main reforming administration (1874–80).

Chamberlain was backed by Churchill and in tandem they were an effective combination. Both had had famous fathers known for their dynamism and enterprise, and now the sons cooperated in a way that their elders had never been able to do, to launch a series of reforming initiatives. The Chancellor made the means available, and it was Chamberlain who drew up and supervised the proposals.

Chamberlain's Reforms

Perhaps Chamberlain's most important achievement was the 1925 Widows, Orphans and Old Age Contributory Pensions Act, in which he showed mastery of the detailed complexities of the legislation. Under the non-contributory arrangements introduced in 1908, pensions were inevitably costly, but the Labour Party was committed to their principle. Chamberlain established contributory pensions for the groups involved. His scheme was to be financed by equal contributions from employers and employees, with an elastic state subsidy to meet expenditure. The Act covered all insured workers by 1937, and with 20 million pounds in the pensions scheme, included equal numbers to the health scheme. He was thus the architect of a programme which survived intact until after the Second World War, and he firmly established the principle of insurance and the importance of contributions as the linchpin of social policy.

We have seen that Chamberlain's interest in local government was long-standing. Indeed, Lloyd George wrote him off as a 'good mayor of Birmingham in an off year'. As Minister of Health, he inherited a confused pattern of local government, parts of which had accumulated at periodic intervals after 1888. The Poor Law was run by Boards of Guardians, and various ad hoc bodies needed sorting out – as did the organisation of health. In 1925, he was responsible for the Ratings and Valuation Act, which was to be the necessary forerunner of a more massive reorganisation of local government. Once the financial arrangements for the funding of local councils were available, then the further reform could proceed.

The new statute was a complex measure, the aims of which were to remove the rating powers of the Poor Law Guardians, produce a single basis for rating valuation and make provision for regular, five-yearly revaluations. The rating system, from which local councils received much of their income, was greatly in need of rationalisation, and the Act which Parliament passed greatly reduced the number of authorities which could levy rates. It replaced some 12,000 parish officials with 648 new rating authorities. The 600 Poor Law Boards responsible in the past for appointing these officials were themselves replaced by 343 regional rating assessment areas. This was a major recasting of the rating system, and it created something like a uniform rating system throughout the country, with a new and up-to-date pattern of valuation.

Most Poor Law Boards had disappeared as a result of the Act, but Chamberlain was caught up in another contentious debate as the result of the Poor Law Guardians. Those in Poplar, in London, and some other authorities under Labour control, paid higher amounts of Poor Law relief than those recommended by the Minister of Health. He acted to check such over-spending by introducing the Guardians Default Act in 1926. This did not resolve the problems for in Poplar councillors were already being surcharged (made personally liable for debts caused by the over-spend) because of their earlier generosity. After a bitter dispute, he produced another measure, the Audit (Local Authorities) Act of 1927, to disqualify any councillor who had over-spent public money. The episode was a difficult one for Chamberlain, and his reputation suffered as a result of 'Poplarism'. He was unenthusiastic about using his powers to act against councillors who exceeded the guidelines, but in the parliamentary rows over the issue his attitude was depicted as mean-spirited.

Reform of the Poor Law had been mooted in the findings of a Royal Commission in 1909, but had never been carried out. Baldwin knew it was a controversial issue to tackle, and Birkenhead felt that 'in my opinion, it is far too disputable and ambitious for any hope that it will reach the Statute Book this session. Personally, I doubt its ever getting there.' Others in the Cabinet feared the possibility of unpopularity resulting from any reform, even if they conceded the merits of the case.

In 1929, in a triumphant measure of rationalisation, the Local Government Act made a clean sweep. The remaining Boards of Guardians were abolished and their powers transferred to Public Assistance Committees of the counties and county boroughs. A neat, simple pattern was created. The 62 counties and 84 county boroughs became the sole authorities under the Ministry of Health for almost all local activities, and overall the number of authorities fell from 11,435 to 10,047. Extensive alterations were made in the areas and functions of local authorities by the Act's 138 sections and 12 schedules.

The Minister of Health had done much to improve local government, and *The Times* recognised his good work by describing the 1929 Act as 'one of the outstanding legislative achievements of the twentieth century'. It gave the credit for the measure largely to Chamberlain, though Baldwin provided solid backing to him again, as he had over rating and all discussion of the Poor Law.

Churchill was keen to see relief given to manufacturers and farmers to assist them with their rate burden. Chamberlain was less convinced for he recognised that local authorities would lose a substantial amount of income they normally derived from the rates. Baldwin agreed to make up the difference by an Exchequer Block Grant, and in 1929, by the Derating of Industry Act (see page 55), agriculture was completely derated, and the burden on industry reduced to one quarter of the general rate.

Chamberlain's work in the field of housing had begun in the 1923 government, and he was keen to shift the country towards greater owner-occupiership. He encouraged a vast building programme of private houses, and also boldly tackled the issue of slum clearance.

Taylor sums up Chamberlain's legislative programme as follows: 'He had efficiency, clarity, resolution; qualities marred only by his unsympathetic manner. It was typical of him that he announced 25 bills to the Cabinet when he took office; typical also that he carried 21.' Yet not all members of that Cabinet were convinced about the wisdom of Chamberlain's policy, and Baldwin's backing in pushing proposals through its discussions was significant. Will the pensions legislation, he, Chamberlain and Churchill had been committed enthusiasts for state action, and all shared a general aim to lessen conflict in society by removing social injustices and making more generous provision for all.

OTHER LEGISLATION

Baldwin's government achieved the passage of a series of notable reforms in various spheres of policy. Two of these were significant measures along the road to collectivism. The Electricity Supply Act of 1926 was passed to rationalise an industry which operated at high costs and low efficiency. There was too much wasteful competition, for many local generating stations at varying frequencies were responsible for producing electricity. Independent enterprises were taken over, and in what amounted to a form of nationalisation a Central Electricity Board was made responsible for generation. The CEB was to establish a national grid for the distribution of electricity, something accomplished by 1933, and which was to prove invaluable when war broke out.

There was some resistance to the Act, not least by the companies who were taken over. Right-wing Conservatives were similarly alarmed, for they scented socialism in the scheme and felt that it created a precedent for further nationalisation along the lines which Labour spokesmen often advocated.

Their suspicions were confirmed in December of that year when another step was taken along the collectivist road. The British Broadcasting Corporation (BBC) was made into a public corporation by royal charter, with the intention that it would provide a single public broadcasting service. The emphasis was to be upon quality programming, and the brief given to those responsible for implementing the charter was that the BBC should 'inform, educate and entertain'. Competition in broadcasting, it was thought, might lead to undue frivolity in programming, and the showing of items of questionable taste.

THE DARK HORSE.

Votes for Women. When all women (including flappers) were to receive the vote, politicians had to win them round. Here, Baldwin, MacDonald and Lloyd George seek to convey a good impression.
Strube (Daily Express)

Critics on the Right were again unhappy. They objected to the exclusion of any element of competition, for they believed in free enterprise. The use of another public corporation, as with electricity, smacked of socialism in their eyes, and the BBC was portrayed as practising a dictatorial paternalism by those who were unrepentant in their commitment to 'true blue' Tory philosophy.

Nor was the Right impressed by the granting of the vote to women over 21, in 1928. By the Representation of the People (Equal Franchise) Act, equality in voting was finally achieved, and all adults who served a three-month residential qualification were entitled to vote. For most people, this was an inevitable final and necessary step in creating a mass democracy, and they welcomed its introduction. Most Conservatives agreed, though they had been prematurely committed to it when the Home Secretary, Joynson-Hicks, promised its introduction in the excitement of a public meeting. Churchill, however, was not convinced by the wisdom of the advance, and Birkenhead and others of his ilk shared such anxieties. As F. E. Smith, he had told the House before the war that 'the total sum of human happiness, knowledge and achievement, would remain unaltered if . . . Sappho had never sung, Joan of Arc had never fought, Siddons had never played, and if George Eliot had never written'. In 1928, his views had not changed, and after the passing of the Bill he remarked that 'The Cabinet went mad yesterday to give the vote to women at the age of 21.' It was only a small rump which took such an obscurantist view of the question, and on the other side of the House there was a feeling that ministers should have gone further and abolished plural voting by which businessmen and graduates were entitled to a second vote.

A final action of the Baldwin government was the resolution of the boundary dispute between Northern Ireland and the Irish Free State. When Lloyd George had conjured up a settlement of the Irish problem in 1922 by persuading the southern Irish to accept partition, he had implied that in a boundary review in 1925 the boundaries of the northern province might be curtailed so that it became unviable. This would have opened up the possibility of a united Ireland.

The Commission set up in 1924 spent a year examining the issue, and its findings were likely to be hotly contested by one side or the other. Rather than go through lengthy negotiations again, perhaps accompanied by bloodshed, the possibility of imposing a settlement was considered. The choice was two-fold, to accept the status quo (the division of Ireland into two separate entities) or to impose whatever the Commission recommended, which Baldwin had reason to believe would favour the south. At a meeting between representatives of both sides, the Free State spokesman agreed to accept the existing border, and thus avoid bitter conflict with the north. The Commission was quietly wound up, and the terms of its findings were never made publicly known.

Baldwin emerged with considerable credit for his role in facilitating a peaceful outcome. By his patient diplomacy and the trust he inspired in representatives from either side, he had secured agreement. Relations between all involved were good, and a new cordiality between the leaders of the Free State and Northern Ireland came about. It was not to last, and within the south there was much ill-feeling among those who wanted an all-Irish republic; O'Higgins, who had suggested that the border be left unchanged, was shot by gunmen soon afterwards.

DEFENCE AND FOREIGN AFFAIRS

Whereas MacDonald was interested in foreign policy and anxious to make an impact as an international statesman, Baldwin had little interest in or understanding of such matters. His choice of Foreign Secretary was therefore all the more important and Austen Chamberlain proved to be an effective appointment, for he possessed a good brain, admirable negotiating ability and genuine interest. Moreover, he was respected in the capitals of Europe.

An early Low cartoon depicted Baldwin rearranging the furniture for his new Cabinet, and Austen Chamberlain was drawn as a rigid lampstand. The image caught something of the personality of the Foreign Secretary, for he was rather stiff and unbending, and prone to vanity. He and Baldwin were never on very close terms, perhaps because both were conscious that Chamberlain had been a former leader of the party at a time when Baldwin was only a junior minister. They never met at Astley, and Chamberlain rarely went to Chequers.

The Foreign Secretary had a relatively free hand to do as he pleased, for Baldwin had expressed his confidence that 'I never need derive worry about foreign affairs, and feel perfectly confident in the judgement and wisdom of the Foreign Secretary.' Chamberlain was secure in the knowledge that the Prime Minister was keen to delegate responsibility but would back him should the necessity arise: 'I wish I could be helpful, but I am not up in the . . . matter. Whatever you do, I will support you', wrote Baldwin in 1927. Chamberlain recognised Baldwin's lack of knowledge and interest: 'He leaves me to go my own way, assume my own policy and face my own difficulties . . . I suspect he feels that he knows less than nothing about foreign affairs . . . sometimes, I wish that he showed a little more enthusiasm.' Most of the time he seemed content that the Prime Minister could count on his experience and expertise, and the backing was there when necessary. Baldwin was willing to defend his Foreign Secretary in his absence, and do his best to neutralise opposition as it arose.

The twin aims of foreign policy in the 1920s involved the search for security and disarmament. Ramsay MacDonald was committed to both, and was particularly keen to see disputes settled around the conference table in order to bring about a real improvement in international relations. As part of an attempt to give teeth to the machinery of the League of Nations, he was keen to promote the Geneva Protocol. This provided for compulsory arbitration of problems between the signatory powers of the League of Nations, pledged them to disarm by agreement and to assist each other in the face of unprovoked aggression. The Conservatives believed that it was a sweeping commitment which could have made Britain a guarantor of every European frontier. In March 1925, Chamberlain rejected the Protocol, claiming amongst other things that the Dominions were unenthusiastic about it.

The Treaty of Locarno

Labour had a stronger belief in the League of Nations as a forum for conciliation than the Conservatives and was willing to enter into commitments of a non-military kind to increase its effectiveness. Some Conservatives were hostile to any such machinery, but Austen Chamberlain saw the need to provide some alternative to the Protocol to satisfy the British public that the Tories were interested in promoting European security. Like MacDonald, he was wary of any agreement under which the burden of any action would fall on British naval power, for the government did not wish to place Britain in the position of policing the world. However, as his contribution to European security, he did wish to take a step to reconcile France and Germany. The means was to be the Treaty of Locarno, signed in October 1925, and immediately recognised as an important step in establishing European peace.

Stresemann, the German Foreign Secretary, welcomed Chamberlain's suggestion of 'special arrangements in order to meet special needs'. They and Briand, the French Foreign Minister, were the prime movers in producing the Locarno Pact which was more modest in scope than the Protocol had been. It confirmed the frontiers laid down at Versailles: Germany, France and Belgium agreed to resolve any disputes by negotiation, and the Italians and British were to act as guarantors of the arrangements, in the event of any violation. No commitment was made for the areas of Europe east of the Rhine, but the demilitarisation of the Rhineland was confirmed.

For all of its limitations – particularly the lack of any coercive sanctions to enforce the agreement and its concentration on security in western Europe – the Treaty was widely viewed as an important step forward. It seemed as though the countries of Europe were willing to live peacefully together and there was a spirit of optimism on the continent. This resurgence of hope for a new era of peace and reconciliation earned Chamberlain the plaudits of many contemporaries in Britain and abroad, and marked the high watermark of his career. For his services to easing tension in international relations, he was granted the Knighthood of the Garter. He was happy to accept the bulk of the credit, and wrote that he was particularly pleased that the King and the Prime Minister were aware that 'it was my policy. That is true, it was mine in conception and still more mine in execution.'

Colleagues in the Conservative Party were grateful that Britain was not to be too closely involved in the affairs of the continent, especially those of Eastern Europe. They were also pleased as ministers to be associated with an obvious success, and Baldwin expressed a general view when he portrayed Locarno as 'the symbol and the cause of a great amelioration in the public feeling of Europe'. Chamberlain himself spoke of 'knitting together the nations most nearly concerned and whose differences might lead to a renewal of strife, by means of treaties framed with the sole object of maintaining as between themselves an unbroken peace'. He saw the Pact as 'the real dividing line between the years of war and the years of peace'.

As part of the agreement, Germany was welcomed into membership of the League of Nations and thereby restored to the ranks of international respectability. Baldwin saw no conflict between the Pact, with its emphasis on the role of the five powers involved, and Britain's obligations to the League of Nations. He supported the League, though he had doubts about moves to disarmament which it was pursuing.

Baldwin had appointed Lord David Cecil as his Chancellor of the Duchy of Lancaster, with a special responsibility for League affairs. In public, the Prime Minister spoke of the value of the organisation and its ideals, though in practice he was unwilling to accept that British foreign policy could be subordinated to its principles if other countries were willing to cast them aside and act in pursuit of their national goals. Cecil was more inclined to pacifism than Chamberlain, and suspected that the Foreign Secretary was unenthusiastic about the League; relations between the two were uneasy.

The Kellogg-Briand Pact

A further indication of the improved atmosphere in Europe was the signing of the Kellogg-Briand Pact in August 1928. Fifteen powers initially (and eventually 65 in all) signed in Paris a document by which war was renounced as an instrument of national policy. Chamberlain was at first deeply sceptical about the whole exercise, but had no wish to offend the United States. After securing some modifications, he then welcomed it warmly, for cooperation might improve relations between Britain and America which were under some strain over the failure of disarmament talks in Geneva in 1927. However, the value of the Pact was very limited. The terms were not defined, and there was no machinery to implement the worthy aspirations. In the words of Arthur Marwick, it was 'of no greater force than the equally admirable sermon of the preacher who, without detailing precise remedies, was against sin'.

The spirit of the Kellogg-Briand Pact, like that of Locarno, contributed to a heady atmosphere of optimism in Europe. There was a feeling that all was well in international relations, though it was to prove to be an illusion. For the moment, the regular conversations between Chamberlain, Briand and Stresemann seemed to augur well for the future, although the attemps at international disarmament produced many proposals but little action.

Disarmament and Defence Expenditure

At the disarmament talks in Geneva Britain was unwilling to concede naval parity to the US and Japan, and there was much bickering over the number of cruisers which each country should maintain. Cecil was so disappointed with the British approach to disarmament that he resigned after the breakdown in negotiations. He felt that Britain was unwilling to concede parity to make a serious move to disarm. His resignation was embarrassing to the government, and seemed to indicate its lack of support for the League under whose auspices the Geneva meetings had been held.

However, in spite of its misgivings about taking a major step to disarmament, Britain had felt able to reduce its expenditure on defence. As Chancellor of the Exchequer, Churchill was involved in a determined struggle with the Admiralty to keep naval spending under control. There were fierce Cabinet battles over the issue in 1925, during what was known as the 'cruiser crisis'. The First Lord of the Admiralty wanted approval for the construction of six new cruisers, but Churchill, once an advocate of British sea-power, resisted. A compromise was reached, by which seven were to be built, but the destroyer and submarine programmes were put on hold. Overall, Churchill succeeded in his goal, and the years 1924–9 witnessed a continuation of the reduction in the percentage of funds allocated to national defence.

Anglo-Soviet Relations

Two other events were important in overseas policy, the first concerning relations with the Soviet Union. Anglo-Russian relations had been at a low ebb since the successful Bolshevik Revolution in 1917, and fears and suspicion of international Communism were widespread in British governing circles. Churchill was notably anti-Bolshevik, and even the much less excitable Baldwin was not immune from discerning 'Reds under the bed'.

The MacDonald government had worked effectively to improve the relationship with the Russians, and backed up its full diplomatic recognition of the USSR with negotiations on a commercial agreement. Then Chamberlain curtly broke off discussions and a marked animosity developed between London and Moscow. Communist headquarters in London were raided in 1925, and the Russian trading company, Arcos, was similarly 'turned over' less than two years later. The mission was wound up on the grounds of its subversive activities, and many of its members were sent home. The Russian government responded by arresting British agents in Moscow.

Baldwin claimed to have strong evidence of Soviet espionage, and this confirmed his suspicions of the Russians' intentions. For all his dislike of their politics, however, he had no wish to sever trading links which could be in Britain's interests.

The Dominions

A more constructive policy was that adopted towards the Dominions. A committee chaired by Balfour had been engaged in the redefinition of Britain's relations with countries of the Empire. The choice of Balfour was a happy one, it helped to cement Cabinet unity by keeping Balfour, a critic of Locarno, on board. Also, his intellectual gifts made him an ideal choice to unravel the complexities involved in the task.

At the Imperial Conference of 1926, the committee's formula was accepted, namely that Britain and the Dominions were 'autonomous Communities within the British Empire, equal in status . . . united by a common allegiance to the Crown, and freely associated as members of the British Commonwealth of Nations'. This statement of existing realities paved the way for the Statute of Westminster (1931) which formally ratified the relationship of the older Empire countries to the mother country.

The position of India was not included in the deliberations of 1926, but the appointment of Lord Irwin (later Lord Halifax) as the new Viceroy of India was an important move. He wanted to see India acquire Dominion status, and persuaded Baldwin to establish a commission on the subject – in the next decade, Indian affairs were to assume a much greater significance.

THE END OF THE MINISTRY

In the late 1920s, younger Conservatives were frustrated by the torpor of the government in its handling of economic and industrial policy. Boothby, Macmillan and others called for a programme of action and recognised that by then the Cabinet had little or nothing left to offer.

They were looking for an imaginative response involving more state intervention, and were known as the YMCA (the Young Men's Conservative Association).

Meanwhile, the Liberals were offering more imaginative proposals for a bold policy of public works, and Baldwin and his colleagues derided their ideas as wild and impracticable. The economist John Maynard Keynes was bewildered by the government's unwillingness to contemplate any novel solution, and complained that the Prime Minister 'had invented the formidable argument that you must not do anything because it will mean that you will not be able to do anything else'. As the election approached, the Liberals had a platform on which to campaign and their 'Orange Book', with its optimistic title 'We Can Conquer Unemployment', outlined a far-reaching scheme of public works and long-term planning. Largely devised by the fertile mind of Lloyd George, the programme represented a challenge to the Labour and Conservative front benches, but neither party offered much by way of response. Labour broadly followed in the Liberals' path but sounded less convincing, and Baldwin's message offered far less hope than either of the opposing parties were able to do.

1927, 1928 and 1929 were described by G. M. Young as 'the years of decay', and in them Baldwin appeared 'to be little more than an amiable observer of events, at home and abroad, which, even if he had the power, he had no will to direct or control . . . [his government] was sliding into a slumberous exhaustion'. Towards the end, the government certainly lost vitality and a sense of direction, and its authority seemed to ebb away. Local council results and by-elections pointed to the loss of support; in 1927–8, by-elections went particularly badly, for the party lost ten of its own seats. Public confidence was undermined, for there was little indication that ministers were in control of the one issue that mattered most, unemployment. There was too much drift and too little decisive action. The thinking was coming from the other side of the House, and the Conservatives seemed to have lost the intellectual initiative. It was all very well to heap scorn on the Liberals' plans, and Baldwin, Neville Chamberlain and Churchill did so forcefully. The trouble was that their own policies had made so little impact on the problem.

Party organisation had deteriorated in the constituencies, despite reforms at Central Office. Morale among activists had declined, and it was proving difficult to enthuse supporters with the Conservative message. For some years, morale had been declining, and there was evidence of frustration felt by local officials about the quality of leadership they were being given from the centre.

THE 1929 ELECTION AND 'SAFETY FIRST'

Baldwin had held on too long, for his government had lost momentum. Yet he was realistically unable to call an election before 1929, because the legislation to grant the vote to women was only passed in July 1928, and then the electoral registers had to be revised to allow for the many new voters to be included. When he eventually decided to go to the country it was perhaps too late to revive the declining fortunes of the party. But Baldwin believed he would win, for although he knew that neither he nor his colleagues had much to offer for the future, his reputation was an asset which could be exploited. He arranged for the election to take place on 30 May 1929.

The attitude of the government was summed up in its timid slogan for the election, 'Safety First', a phrase which completely misjudged the mood of the voters. It was produced by an advertising agency as a reference to a contemporary Ministry of Transport road sign ('Take care before crossing the road'), and even Baldwin was unimpressed by it, but did not seek to overrule the choice. To him and many others, its topicality seemed less important than its lack of inspiration. With serious unemployment, people were looking for a more positive message.

For the campaign, the party did rely on Baldwin's considerable personal appeal, and used large placards of him in a supposedly reassuring pose. It also produced 10,000 copies of a gramophone record entitled 'Stanley Boy', based on the popular hit of the day, 'Sonny Boy'. Baldwin was unenthusiastic about this as well, and a glance at the lyrics suggests reasons for his reaction:

> England for the Free; Stanley Boy!
> You're the man for me; Stanley Boy!
> You've no way of knowing,
> But I've a way of showing,
> What you mean to me; Stanley Boy!

In spite of their innovatory electioneering techniques, the tone imparted by the Conservative campaign leaders was too complacent. They emphasised the recovery in trade and tried to appeal on the basis that they had created a new era of prosperity. They could offer their record, and showed how the curves of production, wages and living standards were steadily rising. They had seen the country through difficult times and led it towards a better future. Although Baldwin held out the hope of more social legislation on topics such as slum clearance and maternity benefit, he generally stressed the impracticality of the proposals of his opponents: 'Mr Lloyd George has made a statement that the Liberal Party is the party of promise. I accept that, and I am not a competitor . . . it is no new thing for a party of performance to be charged with an inadequate programme.'

The electorate was nearly 29 million, the largest it had ever been, for all women could vote for the first time. Of the 76.1 per cent of voters who turned out, more did so for the Conservatives than for Labour. But this was one of those rare elections when the party with the most votes lost in the battle for seats. The Conservatives amassed 8,656,473 votes to Labour's 8,389,512, with 5,308,510 for the Liberals, yet in the distribution of seats Labour had 287, 26 more than the Conservatives, with the Liberals trailing on 59.

Baldwin's appeal had proved insufficient. This time, unlike in 1924, there was no late issue to make people anxious about the Labour Party; indeed, quite the opposite, for they received revised rate assessments under the recent Local Government Act, and these were for many people a nasty shock. Baldwin took defeat badly, more so than in any other election he fought. He took it personally, and though he was not disposed to bitterness he felt surprised that the public should have rejected the performance of his government.

Whereas Baldwin had remained in office after his defeat in 1923 to await the judgement of Parliament, this time circumstances were different. Then the Conservatives had been the largest party. On this occasion, Baldwin resigned after a few days' consideration, and Labour took over to form a second minority government. He recognised that although no party had won outright, nonetheless there was a clear indication that the country had had enough of the Conservatives. He ignored the hopes entertained by Austen Chamberlain of some deal with the Liberals, for 'fusion' had passed its sell-by date and, moreover, any cooperation with Lloyd George would have been anathema to him.

The 1929 election. A Conservative poster points to reviving fortunes.

ASSESSMENT

Baldwin had succeeded in keeping his Cabinet together for the best part of five years, which was an achievement considering the divergent personalities involved. It was a talented front bench team, and it was he who had been able to bring the ex-Coalitionists back into the fold and retain their services. He had kept the same ministers in the same positions as far as possible, for he did not believe in any unnecessary reshuffles.

There was a fund of goodwill towards Baldwin personally among many of the voters, particularly in the period after the General Strike. As one magazine editorial put it: 'Without any calculation, without any ambitious intent, without any effort of self-centred will, he has leapt into a position such as no Prime Minister had occupied since the days of William Pitt.'

Baldwin's performance was often adroit, if low-key, and the style met with disapproval from those who looked for more vigour and dynamism at the top. Certainly within his own party there were many on the Right who had become increasingly disillusioned with the attitude and approach of the government in general and with Baldwin in particular. The personal criticism was, as Rhode James puts it: 'that he did not "lead his Government", that he waited upon events, was vacillating and was usually unsure of his course'.

The attack underrates his contribution, for his skills were exhibited on several occasions, notably in his handling of the General Strike and in his attitude to a broad range of industrial problems over which he did much to ease the conflict. Yet in his failure to prevent the Trade Disputes Act under party and Cabinet pressure, and in his approach to unemployment the criticism has some validity. Moreover, there were policy errors such as the return to the Gold Standard which had done much damage to levels of employment.

From the Left the attack was unsurprising. To Lloyd George, it had been a 'torpid, sleepy, barren' ministry. To Macmillan, writing in the *Saturday Review* in November, 'The Conservative Party has no clear policy on immediate problems; it has no clear goal towards which it feels itself to be striving. It has too many "open questions" and too many closed minds.' The *New Statesman* was particularly scathing, describing it as 'the most inefficient and lazy of modern governments'. The Right was less than impressed, and Lord Rothermere spoke for many of that ilk in saying that he found its measures 'semi-socialistic'.

Churchill's verdict is perhaps an appropriate one, for he found it a 'capable and sedate' government, and those who served in it were in a generally self-congratulatory mood when it fell from office. Baldwin felt that the party had achieved a lot, and pointed to the fact that no other government had achieved such a programme of domestic reform, other than the Liberals between 1906 and 1914. Leo Amery noted that 'We all parted very happily voting ourselves the best government there has ever been, and full of genuine affection for SB.'

This was a generous verdict, and as we have seen one not shared by all contemporaries. The *Annual Register* for 1929 observed that:

The fall of the Baldwin Ministry, while hailed with exultation by the progressive parties, was not deeply regretted by the bulk of its own supporters, who found much to criticise in its leading personalities. Mr Baldwin had been more amiable than forcible, and had shown himself too much inclined to wait on events instead of trying to direct them. Mr Churchill had proved himself the most able debater in the party, if not in the House, but as a financier his success had been questionable; he had not fulfilled his promise of reducing expenditure, and he left to his successor a formidable task in the financing of the de-rating scheme.

Critics might concede that within a limited sphere it was a capable ministry in presiding over a range of tasks, though by 1927–8 there were serious signs that the government was losing ground. What it lacked was any answer to the fundamental problem of unemployment, which was the key issue of the age. That it was 'sedate' is hard to dispute, and indeed the criticism of many within the Conservative fold as well as many outside was that this was a sluggish government, its leader too prone to long bouts of inactivity. If one expected leadership from a government, this was not the ministerial team to provide it – hence the frustration of the assembled Conservatives at their 1925 party conference, as they urged their leader, 'On, Stanley, On'.

Yet there were achievements, for a series of constructive reforms had been introduced by Neville Chamberlain, along with several other pragmatic measures to extend votes for women, and reorganise broadcasting and the electricity industry. The establishment of public corporations marks a move to collectivism and is illustrative of the non-doctrinaire, empirical approach adopted by ministers. A genuine attempt had been made to encourage masters and men to pull together in the national interest, and industrial and political strife had been kept at a low ebb. In Ireland, the boundary dispute had been settled, and abroad, in a generally uneventful period, Britain played a part in the twin ideas of support for the League of Nations and the promotion of European reconciliation.

Baldwin's government had given many people in the country what they wanted for much of the time – orderly and peaceful change, in an atmosphere of political and social consensus. A. J. P. Taylor has caught the tone of its achievement, in saying that 'England drew closer together . . . and class conflicts were dimmed.' This was no mean achievement, and it was a further tribute to Baldwin's qualities and attitudes that he was generally able to persuade the diehards in his own party to stop trying to put the clock back and to come to terms with the modern age. He demonstrated that Conservatives were not averse to using the power of the state to tackle problems, when there was a clear case for change. In the mid-1920s, Conservatism had taken on a more reforming ethos.

timeline	1924	Prime Minister again
	1925	'Peace in our Time' speech
		Set up Samuel enquiry into coal dispute
		Resolution of Irish border dispute
		Locarno Treaty
	1926 May	General Strike
	1927	Trade Disputes Act
	1928	Kellogg-Briand Pact
	1929	Election defeat on 'Safety First' platform

Points to Consider

1) 'Although he preached social reconciliation, he did little to promote it by his policies between 1924–9.' Is the charge against Baldwin unfair?
2) What qualities did Baldwin and Neville Chamberlain respectively bring to the task of carrying through a programme of social improvement?
3) Why was Baldwin an eminently appropriate politician to handle the situation posed by the General Strike?
4) How much attention should we pay to Lloyd George's criticism of this ministry as 'torpid, sleepy, barren'?

4

OPPOSITION AND OFFICE, 1929–35

When Baldwin's government left office in 1929 there was no deep regret among Conservatives. Many of them were disillusioned and the mood of the party was fractious. It thrived on electoral success, of which there had been plenty in the past, and found defeat hard to accept. As on previous occasions, the leader was made the scapegoat. Baldwin had been fortunate to survive in 1923, but now he had led the party to defeat twice in six years. He and those who were his political associates came under attack. J. Davidson, the Party Chairman, was blamed for organising an uninspiring campaign but the bulk of the criticism fell on Baldwin. The campaign had been built around him, and so the defeat was seen as a verdict upon his personal performance.

Baldwin recognised the feelings of disappointment and resentment, and in July he reviewed the situation and told his audience that it was natural that in a moment of defeat there should be a little heart-searching, for everyone was 'a little tired, and a little strained, and nerves [were] a little on edge'. But, he added, 'this is not a time to ask for the head of anyone on a charger; and I for one am not going to cut off any head to put on it'. As for himself, he realised that he held his position only as long as he retained the goodwill of party activists. If this was withdrawn, he would vacate his office and 'go right out of politics'.

Not everyone in the party, however, saw the Conservative defeat in 1929 in the way that he did. Many felt more than a 'little tired', and wanted not just a rest after their hectic campaigning but a change. They would have been quite willing to withdraw the consent of which Baldwin spoke, but at the time there was no powerful rival or obvious successor. As a contemporary sympathiser, Wickham Steed explained: 'The Conservative front-benchers are a scratch lot, with some 'duds' and some 'talents' among them; but not one of them would the Party unanimously prefer to Mr Baldwin.' Neville Chamberlain was not yet viewed as a natural candidate to take up the inheritance; he lacked popular appeal.

'Divided, disgruntled and confused', according to Austen Chamberlain, the party was unsure of which way to move. Harold Macmillan noted that it had 'no clear policy on immediate problems; it [had] no clear goal towards which it feels itself to be striving'. Many Conservatives had for some time been unhappy about the direction in which Baldwin had been leading them. They particularly disliked the 'neo-socialism' of his measures of public ownership, his unwillingness to lay into the Labour Party and trade unionists, and what they regarded as a general lack of drive. They were looking for a more partisan variety of Conservatism which was clearly distinctive from the policies of the other parties.

Baldwin was not a natural Leader of the Opposition, and neither was he very successful in the role. He was conciliatory, whereas supporters wished to see the government harassed at every turn. While he was anxious to be reasonable, they were less concerned about fairness and wanted a more devastating onslaught on ministers.

If the political situation was unclear after the election, it was to become more so as time went by, for the divisions between the parties were not clearcut, and often the bitterest criticism came from within their own organisations rather than from their opponents. Conservative dissensions mirrored those of the Liberal and Labour parties, and they centred upon the issue of protection and, more immediately, upon dissatisfaction with the leader. There was a determined and prolonged attempt to remove Baldwin, who was blamed for failing to make party policy distinctive to the electorate.

THE PRESS LORDS: IMPERIAL PREFERENCE AND INDIA

The challenge to Baldwin was thrown down by the press lords. Lord Beaverbrook of the *Daily Express* was by nature a crusader and his cause was 'Empire Free Trade'. It was, in his view, time for the Empire to show solidarity and unite against a hostile world in which tariff barriers were being erected by almost every country. More convinced protectionists in the party, such as Neville Chamberlain and Leo Amery, were attracted to the idea of imperial preference and to Beaverbrook's agitation.

Sensing trouble, Baldwin acted with unusual speed to reach an accommodation with those who challenged accepted tariff policy. He inclined to their view, but was unwilling to commit himself to taxes on food which would be very unpopular. He knew that the Dominion governments were unenthusiastic about Beaverbrook's ideas, for they had already erected their own tariff barriers. So he made sympathetic remarks about the importance of the unity of the Empire, political and economic. However, his overtures were too vague for Beaverbrook, and were insufficient to stave off further criticism. Lord Rothermere of the *Daily Mail* also took up the Empire theme, and he was particularly personal in his attacks on the policy of the leadership.

Baldwin was placed under unremitting pressure to move in the direction the proprietors wanted, for as they intensified their campaign they pursued him with sustained and unprecedented virulence. This was a time when the claim of newspaper magnates to have a formidable influence on public opinion was taken seriously, and the proprietor of the *Express* particularly was accustomed to being treated with respect and fear. Baldwin was less compliant than they would have liked, and they felt that he should make way for someone more willing to bend to their wishes.

In early 1930, the Conservative Party put up a by-election candidate who opposed the proprietors' outlook, and this goaded them into outright opposition. Beaverbrook refused to stand on the same platform as Baldwin, and through the United Empire Party which they formed, the press lords kept up a personal attack upon him. Davidson was sacrificed as Party Chairman, but his resignation did nothing to lessen the storm. There were real doubts about Baldwin's survival.

Indian events proved another cause of opposition. Sir John Simon had been asked to head a commission on the government of India in 1927. No Indians were represented in the investigation and by way of protest no leading figures of the nationalist Congress Party would give evidence to it. Before it reported in June 1930, the Viceroy, Lord Irwin (a Baldwin appointment) spoke out in support of eventual Dominion status for India, describing it as 'the natural issue of India's constitutional progress'.

Baldwin did not deny the inevitability of such an outcome, though he lamented the timing of his friend Irwin's remarks. Like Irwin, he believed in accommodating the Indians rather than confronting them.

The commission recommended self-government in the provinces, with significant powers remaining in the Viceroy's hands. There was much to discuss, and round table conferences were held against a background of civil disobedience by Indian nationalists who were determined to press for outright independence as their ultimate goal.

Irwin's declaration had been greeted with fervent opposition by many Conservatives and Baldwin was considered closer to the Viceroy and the Labour Party over India than he was to them. Indeed, he was emphatic in his support for MacDonald's round-table approach. Churchill disagreed entirely with conciliation, and denounced Dominion status. He launched into personal denunciations of Gandhi, the frail but astute Indian leader who was the guiding force in the campaign of non-violent civil disobedience: 'Gandhi-ism and all it stands for will, sooner or later, have to be grappled with and finally crushed.'

Churchill attacked Baldwin in the Commons and then left the Shadow Cabinet in January 1931. India provided the immediate reason for his withdrawal, but in reality it was one of a series of issues on which he found his leader wanting. He later expressed his idea of a Conservative Opposition: it 'should strongly confront the Labour Government on all great imperial and national issues, should identify itself with the majesty of Britain as under Lord Beaconsfield and Lord Salisbury, and should not hesitate to face controversy, even though that might not immediately evoke a response from the nation'.

Baldwin made some of his finest speeches on the handling of the Indian question; he always seemed able to rise to the occasion when the issue was an important one. One such speech was made in early March 1931. At a time when the leadership issue was by no means resolved, he addressed the House on Britain's responsibilities. He had been advised to take a conciliatory line with his critics, but he decided to strike out independently and speak as he felt. He told his fellow MPs that, '. . . the Empire . . . It is organic and alive, in a constant process of evolution, a process which is being speeded up every day . . . it cannot be supposed that, in this world of evolution, India alone is static.' He then went on to speak with some frankness about the difficulties within his party, and recognised that there were 'a large number of people in this country who are genuinely apprehensive of all that is going on, and it so happens that they all belong to our party'. But to him

. . . the constitutional government of India [was] by far the most important Imperial question . . . Difficult as the course is, the dangers do not come from the difficulties; they come from extremists in India and at home. I will tell you what I mean. I am firmly convinced that such writings as appear in such papers as the *Daily Mail* will do more to lose India for the British Empire, will do more to cause a revolutionary spirit, than anything else that can be done in any way by anyone else.

It was a speech of great bravery, and Baldwin sat down to tumultuous cheering. It won him much respect and confirmed his reputation in the House. It helped him to re-establish mastery over his own party. However, orations even of this calibre and boldness did not meet with the approval of those Conservatives who detected signs of the beginning of the end of British rule in India. Many of those critics were also the same people who were harrying Baldwin over imperial preference.

Neville Chamberlain was not alone in his feeling that Baldwin was showing too little regard for party opinion in the pursuit of his consensual policies over India. At the time of Churchill's departure in January 1931 he had written that 'The question of the leadership is again growing acute.' Amery agreed, and told Chamberlain that Tory opinion in the country was apprehensive about Baldwin's approach. Shortly afterwards (26 February 1931), the principal agent of the party, Sir Robert Topping, drew up a memorandum expressing the view that there was alarm in the constituencies.

The document, sent to Chamberlain in his new capacity as Party Chairman, suggested that 'our supporters are worried about the question of India. They lean more towards the views of Mr Churchill than to those expressed by Mr Baldwin in the House of Commons'. But Topping felt that there was little backing for a change of leadership, unless it was 'on a broad policy and not on any single issue'. He was seemingly keen for Baldwin to depart, although he was doubtful about Churchill's suitability as a successor – the more so as he was a free trader. Chamberlain was aware that he did not suffer this disadvantage, and after deleting a couple of 'too wounding' phrases he delivered the memorandum to Baldwin on 1 March. He also tendered the advice that a number of eminent Conservatives felt it was time for him to depart, and Baldwin seemed disposed to acquiesce.

THE DEFEAT OF THE PRESS LORDS

The assault on the leadership raged throughout 1930 and by early 1931 the tone of the dispute had notably sharpened. Baldwin twice found it necessary to seek support from his backbenchers at a party meeting, to shore up his position. In June 1930, Rothermere had demanded that he should be consulted about the composition of any future Conservative government, and at one of these two meetings Baldwin responded to criticism and told his assembled audience: 'We are told that there is a crisis . . . there will be a crisis if you cannot make up your minds . . . You have been told that we have no policy. We have a policy that I have been explaining up and down the country.' As for the press lords, Baldwin played a skilful hand. He read out the relevant extracts from Rothermere's letter, and then added that when he was sent for by the King to form a future government he would have to say: 'Sire, these names are not necessarily my choice, but they have the support of Lord Rothermere.' He repudiated his impertinence with contempt, and dismissed such behaviour as that of an 'insolent plutocracy'. The ultimatum was 'both ludicrous and unconstitutional'.

The occasion was a triumph for Baldwin, and that afternoon, in the Chamber of the House of Commons, he was warmly received, not least by his Labour opponents. Harold Laski wrote to commend his brave stand, and praised him for his devotion to the 'peaceful evolution of English politics'. Many MPs resented the attempt of the press to dictate the course of policy and the choice of personnel by attacking Baldwin's leadership in the way they were doing. However, as G. M. Young later wrote: 'a referendum taken on personality would have given Baldwin 100 votes to Beaverbrook's 10; taken on policy, taken in the party – the numbers would be nearer even'. There were indeed still many doubters in the party, and though Baldwin had temporarily regained command the issue of the leadership was not permanently resolved.

After a brief lull, the campaign against Baldwin renewed. As we have seen, in early March 1931, Baldwin was on the verge of retirement, after Neville Chamberlain had conveyed the feeling that it was time for the leader to go. Chamberlain was confident that he had achieved his object, and *The Times* had an article ready to print entitled 'Mr Baldwin Withdraws'. But at a private meeting, Baldwin was persuaded to 'stand

and fight', and his wife encouraged him with the unlikely phrase, 'Tiger Baldwin'; at the last moment, he decided to fight back.

Matters were brought to a head by a by-election in the safe seat of St George's, Westminster. The Empire Free Traders ran a candidate, and Duff Cooper came forward to resist them as the representative of the leadership. Baldwin spoke in his support on 17 March 1931, and used the occasion to denounce his press critics. He was scornful of Beaverbrook and Rothermere whose behaviour had caused him so much difficulty, and he flayed them for their tendentious and selective reporting. He castigated their papers with his rebuke:

> They are engines of propaganda for the constantly changing politics, desires, personal wishes, personal likes and dislikes, of two men. What are their methods? Their methods are direct falsehood, misrepresentation, half-truths, the alteration of the speaker's meaning by publishing a sentence apart from the context, such as you see in these leaflets handed out inside the doors of this hall; suppression and editorial criticism of speeches which are not reported in this paper. These are methods hated alike by the public and by the rest of the Press . . . What the proprietorship of these papers is aiming at is power, and power without responsibility – the prerogative of the harlot throughout the ages.

The final phrase was the one which made the headlines. It had been suggested by Baldwin's cousin, Rudyard Kipling, and in the words of Rhode James, it 'electrified the audiences and a wider public'. If popular opinion was with Baldwin, the speech earned him the undying enmity of the Beaverbrook and Rothermere papers. But it achieved its objects; Duff Cooper proceeded to a convincing victory, and Baldwin had saved his leadership. Beaverbrook remarked that: 'He always beats me – the toughest and most unscrupulous politician you could find – cold, merciless in his dislikes.' Shortly afterwards, he agreed on a truce with Baldwin and other critics were silenced.

Baldwin could be deadly in his reactions. He chose his moment, and in this most memorable of his speeches, laid into the personal failings of his opponents. In so doing he fortified his position. Churchill later wrote of Baldwin's 'phlegmatic capacity of putting up with a score of unpleasant and even humbling situations in order to be master of something very big at the end of a blue moon'. He had a point, and certainly Baldwin was 'strong on the rebound', when provoked. Although sporadic criticism from the Right continued and he was often placed under pressure, there was no further challenge and his leadership was not in danger for several years.

Neville Chamberlain, who had harboured hopes of taking over, had to bide his time. He was frustrated by Baldwin's performance and would have liked to see the same energy used against the Labour Party as was used against the press. However, by placing him in the position of Party Chairman, Baldwin had acted shrewdly and protected his leadership from a possible Chamberlainite coup. It would have been difficult for Chamberlain or his supporters to act, without seeming disloyal.

Chamberlain's precise role at this difficult time in Baldwin's career is unclear. Many years ago, an early biographer, Keith Feiling, recorded that: 'Great was the realm of temptation spread before him by other considerable persons.' The research of Middlemas and Barnes led them to take a generally charitable view of his behaviour over the 'Topping Memorandum', and to claim that he acted honourably. Roy Jenkins was more severe, and wrote of how 'Chamberlain behaved somewhat unctuously, showing [the Topping Memorandum] to half the Shadow Cabinet, in order to get their advice on whether or not he ought to worry Baldwin about it.'

The recollections of Baldwin and Chamberlain were at variance as to what happened on 1 March. Chamberlain claimed that Baldwin told him he intended to depart, and then asked his Chairman how his colleagues would react. Baldwin recalled having told Chamberlain that he was under some pressure to go, and had asked him for his own verdict – to which he had answered that he should quit the leadership, and that other prominent Conservatives were of a similar view. But whichever came first, Baldwin's willingness or Chamberlain's recommendation, there was little doubt that Baldwin lacked full-hearted support from his Chairman who was displeased with the decision to carry on. Nevertheless, in spite of the considerable temptation to pursue a course designed for his personal benefit, Chamberlain held back from any direct assault. If he had tried to exploit the weakness of the leader's position and make a direct leadership bid, he would probably have lost and damaged his future prospects by having appeared to be lacking in loyalty and honour. He resigned the Chairmanship in March after only nine months. Much as he was eagerly awaiting his chance to take control of the party, the time was not yet ripe.

For Baldwin, 1931 was 'the year when my party tried to get rid of me'. His prestige in the House and his popular following in the country were still considerable, but for a time he had been very vulnerable. The campaign against him was never strong in the House, where most Conservative MPs were not involved in any manoeuvres to force him to stand down. The threat was said to have derived from the 'country', in whose name the newspaper proprietors claimed to speak. Politicians of the time took the position of these men seriously, but they tended to overrate their own power. Their tactics had backfired, and whatever the views of Conservative activists most fair-minded people felt far more sympathy for Baldwin than they ever did for press lords who had an inflated impression of their own importance.

The most acute phase of Conservative disunity and the moment of Baldwin's greatest danger had passed. His authority was restored sufficiently for him to play an important role in the events which followed in August 1931.

THE SECOND LABOUR GOVERNMENT, 1929–31

The overriding issue which dominated the short existence of the second Labour government was unemployment, for it was the party's misfortune to be in office during the most acute phase of the Great Depression. As in 1924, Labour ministers had no more of a solution to the problem than did the Conservatives. Although members on the left of the party urged a specifically socialist approach, MacDonald behaved in much the same way as a more avowedly capitalist prime minister would have done.

In October 1929, the Wall Street Crash broke out and although for a while its impact on the British economy was not serious, by early 1931 the situation was acute. The government was overtaken by a world slump which was to have a prolonged and catastrophic impact on industry and agriculture throughout the world. In Britain, unemployment rose sharply, the unemployment fund fell into serious deficit and the country's gold reserves were threatened. Snowden, again at the Treasury, set up an Economy Committee packed with orthodox thinkers and chaired by Sir George May. It reported in July and produced a gloomy analysis of the country's finances. Its recommendations were in line with conventional economic wisdom and involved strict economies in national expenditure.

A sterling crisis developed and as gold flowed out of the country, MacDonald returned from his holiday on 11 August. During the twelve days of crisis which followed, there was a widespread recognition of the need to restore confidence, and in addition to the consultations between the Bank of England and members of the Cabinet, there was regular contact with opposition leaders. A package of economy measures was envisaged and this was the issue which caused disarray in the government. Cuts of 56 million pounds were provisionally agreed, but in order to secure a loan from the American bankers, J. P. Morgan, further savings of 12.5 million pounds were seen as necessary: a 10 per cent reduction in unemployment benefit was the means by which this was to be achieved. Although most of the Cabinet could accept this, a minority was unwilling to acquiesce. MacDonald decided on resignation and informed the King accordingly.

THE FORMATION OF A NATIONAL GOVERNMENT

It was the monarch's duty to find a prime minister and ensure that government could carry on, and in normal circumstances, George V would have sent for Baldwin as the leader of the second largest party. However, the King persuaded MacDonald to continue as head of a National Government – a decision which soon landed MacDonald in difficulty with his party, the bulk of which was opposed to the idea. The other parties were in ready agreement and so on 24 August a Conservative-dominated administration was formed in which, other than the Prime Minister, there were only four Labour figures.

How Did the National Government Come About?

Of course the key was the intractable financial situation, but two other factors concerned the state of the party system and the personalities involved. In the late 1920s, Labour was replacing the Liberals as the main alternative to the Conservatives, but the older progressive party was still large enough to deny any party an overall majority. In addition, the two largest parties were faced with internal schism. Labour had a dissident left wing which had little faith in the orthodoxies of the MacDonald leadership, whilst among the Conservatives there was deep hostility towards Baldwin from influential Tories following his electoral failure in

1929. Within this disruption to the normal smooth operation of the two-party system there was sporadic talk on both Left and Right of a cessation of hostility throughout the period 1929–31.

In the press there was speculation about the merits of politicians 'sinking their differences' in a spirit of national unity, and the editor of the *Observer*, J. L. Garvin, was calling for such cooperation from early in 1931. In December 1930, a Low cartoon had gone further and with remarkable prescience had depicted MacDonald at the Cabinet table with Baldwin sitting in close attendance, the drawing accompanied by the caption: 'The Unemployment question having produced a crisis, Mr MacDonald forms a National Government'. Moreover, the principal figures involved in the dramatic events of August 1931 were temperamentally disposed to coalition. The King was receptive to a display of unity in time of national difficulty, and the two main party leaders were willing to follow the suggestion put to him by the Liberal,

Members of the newly-formed National Government preen themselves, sporting white feathers.

Samuel, for an all-party government under MacDonald's continued leadership. Samuel saw him before Baldwin who would normally as the leader of the largest party, have gone in first. But Baldwin could not be found, and so the suggestion was made. The King responded with enthusiasm, and by the time the Conservative leader arrived he was asked whether he would be willing to serve. As he later remarked; 'In the circumstances of that meeting, and at that time, there was nothing for anyone in my position to do but promise full cooperation to tide over this crisis whatever it might involve'.

After the Government was formed, the King was to speak of it as 'not . . . a coalition in the ordinary sense of the term, but cooperation of individuals'. The two principal individuals got along well, and Baldwin admired MacDonald and found him a kindred spirit in many of his attitudes. Moreover, he knew that some Conservatives were openly canvassing the idea of cooperation at Westminster, but felt that the party 'would not stand it for a moment'. In July 1931, he rejected the notion of an all-party coalition, the main obstacle as he saw it being the question of tariff policy. He believed that tariffs were inevitable and would only cooperate with other parties if the topic was on the agenda. From 1929 Labour and the Liberals had been working together in order to fend off any move to protection.

At this stage, Baldwin was unenthusiastic about serving in a coalition, but he was more willing to contemplate a limited form of cooperation whereby his party would not oppose any necessary measures to defeat the looming crisis. He would 'take a helpful line in Parliament' if suitable policies were brought forward. They would have to be ones which commanded wide agreement, and this involved some dialogue with spokesmen from other parties. After any agreement Labour would have continued to bear the responsibility for devising them and taking them through Parliament. He still thought a Conservative Government would eventually be necessary. He wrote to Chamberlian that; 'I think in the long view it is all to the good that the Government have to look after their own chickens as they come home to roost, and get a lot of the dirt cleared up before we come in.'

Baldwin was certainly not inclined to coalition; he had been the man who had helped to bring down the Lloyd George coalition in 1922. As late as August 22, he gave Hoare the impression that he had no wish to return to office, and 'having destroyed one coalition [did not] wish to form another'. Only as a last resort would he join a National Government, whereas Chamberlain and Hoare were more enthusiastic

In *My Political Life*, Leo Amery noted that Baldwin would have been happy to govern with Liberal support and told the King that he was willing to do so if assured it would be forthcoming. But in fact Baldwin was entirely content for MacDonald to continue. Like Samuel, he preferred to see the Prime Minister stay on and deal with the crisis as a leader of the Labour Party. However, if this was impossible then a MacDonald-led, all-party government was the next best thing.

There was certainly some party advantage in this approach. A Conservative government would have gained little popularity from taking measures necessary to stave off economic disaster and much of the blame would rub off on MacDonald if he remained Prime Minister. He, Baldwin, would be one step removed from the responsibility for action, yet still be seen as responding in the appropriate patriotic manner. Moreover, if MacDonald did stay on, this would be damaging to the unity of the Labour Party and at any forthcoming election, Conservative prospects would be enhanced. Neville Chamberlain was particularly attracted to the idea of an early dissolution, in which Labour would be heavily defeated.

In other words, there was in 1931 a conjunction of circumstances which made some form of coalition seem desirable. Such a government tends to be a strong possibility when there is a national emergency which requires a drastic and painful remedy. It is the more likely when there is a minority administration already in existence, and the action being contemplated is of a type which is repugnant to its own supporters. Not surprisingly, in 1930–1 there were politicians who were ready to contemplate an all-party approach.

Baldwin gave his explanation for the decision to join a National Government on 28 August, and also spoke of the conditions which had been agreed between the parties. He distinguished two problems: balancing the Budget and balancing Britain's trading position, the second being a problem which in his view would necessitate the introduction of protective tariffs. The new government was formed to tackle the budgetary crisis and effect economies, and would deal with such other events as arose during its lifetime. There was agreement to do this between all the parties, but:

After that our agreement ends and we part company . . . the tariff . . . is absolutely essential to complete the work which is being begun by the rectification of the Budgetary finance. When this Parliament dissolves, when the economies are carried and the budget is balanced, you will then have a straight fight on tariffs and against the Socialist Party.

Some Conservatives were worried about the position in which the party was being placed. Amery wrote to *The Times* on the same day, and observed that the leader and other key figures were

inspired by the most patriotic motives, and for reasons which seemed convincing to them, have . . . agreed . . . on the basis of postponing a remedy for the real crisis, in order to patch up the Budget situation . . . Experience shows how difficult it is for a Cabinet to deal with one issue only. New issues arise which must be dealt with, and which each tend to justify the prolongation of a Government's existence and to consolidate it.

Like many others, he could well understand how his party had responded to a national crisis. It could not stand aside, and delay was impossible in the circumstances. But he was anxious to stress the shortness of the partnership as an election loomed.

BALDWIN'S ROLE

As well as acting as MacDonald's deputy, Baldwin took a non-departmental office as Lord President of the Council. He was admirably fitted to the role of principal adviser and despite his apparently uninfluential post he was to prove a key figure. He commanded widespread personal support across the Commons, and he was the leader of the largest party in the Chamber. Without him, Stuart Ball has observed, no National Government would have been possible:

Baldwin's willingness to sit back and leave formal power to Ramsay MacDonald may have been the result of laziness and lack of resolution, but without it, the National Government would hardly have lasted a few months.

A more active Conservative such as Chamberlain would have wanted a prestigious office and may have taken initiatives which would have been unwelcome to his coalition partners. Samuel, who as a leading Liberal and coalition minister worked with him, noted that he was always ready to take the lead: 'His ideas were positive and clear cut; he was tenacious in the pursuit of them . . . [he] was willing to listen to arguments with a friendly spirit – but a closed mind.' By contrast, Baldwin's unassertive style caused few problems for his colleagues; he had few ideas but was open to suggestions. However, his party's dominance ensured that policies eventually adopted were acceptable to his fellow Conservatives.

Baldwin may have been the linchpin of the new arrangement, but he was careful not to usurp prime ministerial authority. He did not seek to 'steal the thunder', and was content to allow others to take the initiative. Samuel noted that 'when a discussion was taking an awkward turn, he would intervene at the end with some brief observation, full of common sense, that helped us to an agreement'. But Baldwin recognised that he was not in charge, and because of his secondary role he cannot be blamed for the failings of the government during MacDonald's premiership. He was a member of the team, a very important member but nonetheless not the man who made the final decisions or who had to take the responsibility for them.

THE ELECTION OF 1931

Neither Baldwin nor MacDonald was keen to hold an early election for there was much internal dissension in all parties about the formation of the coalition. More partisan figures disliked the compromise and moderation implicit in a 'sinking of party differences'. Some Conservatives were particularly keen to see an election in which they could take advantage of Labour divisions, and of close colleagues it was Neville Chamberlain who urged a reluctant Baldwin to seek public approval for what had been agreed between the parties in August 1931. It was Chamberlain who coined the phrase a 'Doctor's Mandate', which meant obtaining the backing of the electorate for the measures necessary to tackle the crisis.

The outcome in October was a massive endorsement of the National Government with Labour down to only 59 seats. Supporters of the

National Government won in 556 of the 615 constituencies, and the Conservatives and their allies alone were victorious in 473 of them. For Baldwin, this was 'no party victory . . . the country has sent out an SOS to the Government, and now we have to rise to it'.

With such parliamentary support, Baldwin could act without any feelings of dependence on his right-wing followers. He proceeded to commit his party to the chosen route of the political consensus rather than to the more partisan Conservatism represented by the press lords.

THE YEARS 1931–5

Baldwin did not immerse himself in the detail of much government policy. However, he was committed to the Statute of Westminster, and smoothed its passage through the House of Commons. This was the measure which finally recognised that the Dominions had grown to keep maturity and were joined with Britain only by ties of sentiment and a common commitment to the Crown. They were granted complete independence, and were to all intents and purposes sovereign states.

Baldwin was also personally involved in the question of India's constitutional evolution, a cause which had landed him in such difficulty in 1930–1. By the Government of India Act in 1935, the most important issues remained in British hands via the Viceroy and his advisers, but many powers were handed over to the provincial governments and the Indian legislatures; in the most advanced provinces, control of the police was handed over as well. Churchill threatened to 'smash the government' during the passage of the Bill, but Baldwin later remarked that he had never intended to be 'smashed'.

In other areas, the government turned to protection and introduced a tariff on goods from overseas. The time for free trade had passed in the economic depression of the early 1930s. Every country turned to quotas and controls of some variety, for none of them felt able to allow in foreign items at the expense of those produced at home. The consequences for unemployment were too serious, and in Britain there were at this time two and a half million out of work.

For the Liberals in the government, protection presented a problem, for some of them could not entertain the idea of a general tariff. In Cabinet, Baldwin made it clear that the majority opinion was in favour of such an imposition, and that if those who believed in free trade resigned then the Conservatives could easily assume the reins of power, and introduce tariffs themselves. A compromise was reached when the unusual constitutional doctrine of an 'agreement to differ' was put forward as a lifeline to those who found it difficult to bend to the wind. Any member of the Cabinet was free not only to speak but actually to vote against the collective view of the government to which he belonged.

For Baldwin, this was the time when he was at last able to pursue the economic policy in which he had long believed. The same was true for Neville Chamberlain, the Chancellor of the Exchequer, who had supported his father's attempt to convert the party and the country to 'tariff reform'. The time was now ripe for an experiment on their terms, and free trade was about to be jettisoned. It had long been the prevailing orthodoxy, but among Conservatives there was a growing feeling that it was time to put forward a distinctive policy based upon protection.

Chamberlain introduced the Import Duties Bill in February 1932. It was designed to place a minimum 10 per cent duty on most foreign goods, but exempted food, raw materials and Commonwealth products. Baldwin summed up the case for such a measure. He argued that tariffs would provide a breathing-space for British industrialists, especially those in iron and steel companies which had suffered severely in the last few years: 'those industries can benefit themselves and the country under the shelter of a tariff, can carry out schemes of reorganisation that can attract capital, and can lay down new plans'. Unemployment would be brought down, for British industry could operate at full time, on the basis of cheaper production.

Baldwin and other Conservatives were hopeful that the Ottawa Conference in July 1932 would take them further along the road of which Joseph Chamberlain had once dreamed, imperial unity. Conservatives often alluded to it in their speeches, but as yet it remained nothing more than rhetoric. Baldwin set out his ideas by saying that he recognised that 'the splitting up of Europe into small self-contained states with high tariffs' was a barrier to trade. He believed that now that Britain had forsaken free trade there was a real chance of bringing about mutual tariff reductions, and the place to start was in Ottawa.

Baldwin led the British delegation, though the Chancellor handled the more detailed work. In addition to Britain, Australia, Canada, India,

South Africa and New Zealand were represented at the conference, all of which now had fiscal autonomy since the passage of the Statute of Westminster. However, whilst they all showed a notional interest in the idea of economic unity within the Empire, the Dominions were less enthusiastic about measures which would have actually promoted such a union. They offered very little to the British negotiators, other than a willingness to raise tariffs against foreign countries and so leave British exporters in a favourable position. This was a kind of preference, but not one based on tariff cuts as a policy of imperial preference usually implied. In return, it was expected that Britain would impose tariffs against foreign countries, but allow in Empire goods without restriction. This would have meant that British people would have paid higher prices for many imported goods, just so that Empire producers could have free access to the British market.

Such an arrangement had little appeal to Chamberlain or Baldwin, who were looking for actual reductions in tariffs. Also, as many British products were sold outside the Empire, there was a prospect that Britain would have suffered an additional problem. Many overseas governments might have imposed additional restrictions by way of retaliation for the discriminatory policies involved in imperial preference. This could have further damaged prospects for exports and employment.

After protracted discussions which came near to collapse, a settlement was eventually reached by which imperial producers received free access to the British market for the bulk of their goods, and Britain promised to retain a tariff against non-Empire countries for ten years. The Dominions made some concessions to allow modest advantages to British exporters, but overall the arrangements were more to the benefit of the Dominions. Ottawa was a disappointment for Baldwin and Chamberlain, and the best that they could claim was that a foundation had been laid on which further amendments towards a more general liberalisation of trade could be based. This, Baldwin felt, was the key to a general revival of world trade.

In September 1932, Snowden and the Liberals took their dislike of the Ottawa Agreement to the point of resignation, and with their departure the government became even more dominated by the Conservative Party. In reality, it was a MacDonald-led Conservative government, with support from a tiny band of National Liberals who felt able to forsake traditional Liberal attitudes and work with their allies after 1931.

Much of the other work in domestic policy was carried out by Chamberlain, whose policies involved help for 'special areas', those industrial regions hardest hit by unemployment in the declining industries. He was responsible for the Unemployment Act, which introduced the idea of 'means-testing' by which a family's assets were assessed as a basis for calculating how much relief it should receive. Housing was also tackled, and the Rent Act was designed to end rent control in the private sector to encourage landlords to make more accommodation available. The building programme also favoured the private market, boosted as it was by a policy of low interest rates. A housing boom got underway, with expansion proceeding at twice the rate of development in other industries. Such progress was helpful not only in tackling the problem of living conditions, it also helped to boost overall consumer demand.

Baldwin was happy to back such measures, for his dislike of the minutiae of detail was even greater than it had been a decade before. Chamberlain's irrepressible desire to solve problems admirably suited his needs. With the Chancellor in charge of policy, Baldwin was able to sit back and concentrate on his personal role. He was Lord President, a job the importance of which varies in individual governments. His view was that it involved more work and less pay than any other he had known. He also acted as Lord Privy Seal, another non-departmental post, between 1932-4, and because of MacDonald's failing powers effectively took over the role as Leader of the House of Commons as well. He increasingly devoted more time to managing the business of the House. Such was the regularity of his appearances on behalf of the government and his popularity in that capacity, that other members came to assume that he had the title in reality, as well as in practice.

Baldwin was a committed parliamentarian, who strongly believed in the democratic values which were under threat from the dictators on the continent. He realised the importance of ensuring that Labour remained wedded to the gradualist route to socialism, and understood that there were embittered members of the party who questioned the value of democratic opposition at a time when there was a National Government with an overwhelming majority. He tried to ensure that Labour was treated with courtesy and consideration, and by so doing encouraged its MPs to retain their faith in the parliamentary process.

THE ADVANCE OF COLLECTIVISM AND ECONOMIC RECOVERY

During the early 1930s the old preference for laissez-faire was increasingly questioned. Free competition and non-interference had broken down, and there was an awareness of the need to regulate prices and output, and 'rationalise' inefficient and ill-equipped industries. This required a new emphasis upon the role of government in a policy of what was sometimes called 'planned capitalism'.

Baldwin was aware that the National Government was moving along the road of growing state intervention in economic activity, something many Conservatives normally preferred to avoid. But he had always been a pragmatist, and the 'Tory collectivism' of his earlier premiership was a recognition of his acceptance of growing interventionism. 'There is no question that the State could do much to provide favourable conditions and that all parties [are] committed to a degree of intervention in the life of the individual that would have [once] seemed excessive or tyrannical', he observed. Competition was seen as less beneficial than cooperation, and by 1939, the British economy was one in which private enterprise worked in partnership with the state. Such 'mixed' policies seemed to provide the best means of escaping from the hazards of the Depression, and after 1932 there was indeed an economic recovery.

The economic performance of the National Government has been viewed very differently by post-war historians. If its name implied an all-party administration, its character was markedly pro-Conservative – even more so after 1932. The decade was one of Conservative hegemony and by the beginning of 1934 only four members of the Cabinet belonged to other parties. In other words, a judgement on the National Government is to a large extent a judgement on the Conservative Party. Left-wing historians generally point to the long queues of the unemployed seeking their dole payment, to the horrors of means-testing and to the failures of rearmament. More sympathetic writers have stressed the fact that the government led Britain out of the slump, affected a major tariff revision, began rearmament despite Labour opposition and made progress towards Indian self-government.

In 1933, Britain began a recovery which reached its peak in 1937. Steady economic growth, rising real wages, new industries catering for the consumer and increased expenditure on social services were the outcome of this revival which was the more impressive given the slow recovery of world trade in general. There is less agreement on the role of the government in promoting this upward cycle. However, what can be said is that in a decade when other countries were turning to Fascism or Communism, Britain remained wedded to the democratic route. Its achievements may have been less dramatic than those of some authoritarian regimes but MacDonald, Baldwin and their colleagues returned the country to better times after the prolonged slump, and did so without sacrificing essential freedoms.

FOREIGN POLICY

The decade of the 1930s was one in which the great questions of peace and war assumed considerable significance. The causes of the Second World War are highly complex and much discussed by historians, but the treatment of Germany in the Versailles Treaty of 1919, the failure of the League of Nations and the weaknesses of British foreign and defence policy under MacDonald, Baldwin and Chamberlain, have all been targets for criticism – even if there is a recognition that the outbreak of hostilities in 1939 owed much to Germany's policy of aggression and expansion after Hitler came to power in 1933.

The era of the MacDonald premiership was to witness a deteriorating international situation, for which many politicians were ill-prepared. The glow of the Locarno settlement seemed a distant memory, and new perils arose on the continent and elsewhere in which democracy was under attack and dictatorship on the increase.

Early in its life, the National Government faced a challenging situation in foreign policy when the Japanese invaded Manchuria, then a part of the Chinese Empire, in 1931. The invasion has been viewed by many people as the first major blow to the League of Nations, but at the time there was little that the British or any other country in the League could do about it. Britain lacked sufficient military strength in the Far East to thwart Japan, which could be seen as an indication that disarmament had gone too far.

In 1932, the Ten Year Rule which had prevented the armed forces from budgeting for war for a decade, was abandoned. However, 1932 did not seem an appropriate moment for rearmament, for a Disarmament

Conference was about to begin. Progress was undermined by the accession to power of Adolf Hitler in January 1933, for he was bent on achieving military equality for Germany, a policy which alarmed France and her eastern European allies who felt vulnerable to German military might. In October, Germany left the Conference.

Baldwin was alarmed by the rise of Nazism in Germany and recognised that 'we are coming to the parting of the ways in Europe'. Churchill was the other leading politician who diagnosed the danger which Hitler posed, though he saw his value as a bulwark against the expansion of international Communism. As for Fascism in Italy, Baldwin had some admiration of what Mussolini had achieved, and neither was he concerned about the aggression of Japan, a state with 'the highest sense of national honour and patriotism'. It was the menace of German militarism which concerned him, but that was yet to be a major issue.

In 1933 there was much support for disarmament, for revulsion at the horror of warfare in 1914–18 remained alive in British minds. In November 1932 Baldwin said that if disarmament failed, it would be because the young were too intent on retaining aeroplanes. He was concerned with the danger presented by aerial bombing, and had tried to get an agreement at the Geneva disarmament talks to lessen the possibility of future air attack. He suggested that 'the bomber will always get through', and expressed his recognition of the horror presented by a world in which there were too many arms: 'The only defence is offence, which means that you have to kill more women and children more quickly than the enemy if you want to save yourselves.'

Pacific sentiment abounded, and this was apparent in February 1933 in a celebrated debate at the Oxford Union. The motion 'This House will in no circumstances fight for its King and Country' was carried, for it appealed to those who were outright pacifists as well as those who believed in the League of Nations. The East Fulham by-election of October 1933 provided a similar message – a Labour candidate fighting on a pacifist platform secured a convincing majority of 4840 in what had been a safe Conservative seat with a 14,521 majority.

The right-wing newspapers of Beaverbrook and Rothermere were sceptical of the value of the League of Nations and in response to their campaigning, the League of Nations Union, a non-party group whose political support spanned pro-League Conservatives, many Liberals and the majority on the centre-right of the Labour Party, organised a massive survey of public opinion in 1935. From the 11 million respondents to this 'Peace Ballot', it was evident that there was strong support for disarmament and for the League. Most responses to Question Five backed economic sanctions if 'one nation insists on attacking another', but in the following question, which involved backing economic measures with military action, the result was a considerable but less overwhelming majority of 6.75 million for and under 2.5 million against.

The effect on the government was to encourage it to downplay rearmament which increasingly looked necessary, and to stress support for the League, albeit with economic sanctions rather than military ones, unless there was a direct threat to British interests. Those who opposed the conduct of foreign policy at this time tended to stress that nearly three-quarters of those who had answered Question Six were in favour of using force, whereas those who defended it pointed to the not insignificant numbers who disagreed with such action.

It was in the same month as the Peace Ballot that Baldwin took over as Prime Minister from Ramsay MacDonald, for what was to be his third and final premiership. By then, he had come to the conclusion that it was too late to think in terms of disarmament. The world had become a significantly more dangerous place, and he could see that it was necessary to take measures to counter the threat to stability that a rearming Germany might pose. The new emphasis must be on defence, especially aerial defence, but convinced of its necessity he did not provide a positive lead by informing the nation of the dangers ahead.

timeline	1929–31		Hostility of press lords
	1930–31		Attacked by Churchill over India
	1931	March	Baldwin attacked press lords in 'Power without responsibility' speech
		August	Sterling Crisis
			Formation of National Government under MacDonald; Baldwin Lord President
		October	Election victory for National Government; Baldwin a 'power behind the throne'
	1935		Resignation of MacDonald as Prime Minister; replaced by Baldwin

Points to Consider

1) Why was there so much hostility to Baldwin on the right of the Conservative Party?
2) What motives led him to back the formation of the National Government in August 1931?
3) In what ways was the position of Lord President of the Council one for which Baldwin's qualities made him singularly well-suited?

5

THE THIRD ADMINISTRATION, 1935–7

In May 1935, MacDonald finally recognised that his premiership had outlived its usefulness. Society had already labelled him as 'Ramshackle Mac', and in his last years he was an ineffectual Prime Minister. His physical powers were markedly diminishing and so was his mind. A rambling if vain old man, he was mocked in the House of Commons by some MPs who viewed his performances with increasing derision.

MacDonald was clearly unfit to lead the government into the next election, and Baldwin was well aware of the decline in his faculties. He later wrote: 'Poor old Ramsay was a doughty fighter in his early days; it was tragic to see him in his closing days as PM, losing the thread of his speech and turning to ask a colleague why people were laughing.' Yet he made no attempt to edge him out of office, for even if he sometimes felt as though MacDonald was 'like an eiderdown wrapped round my head', there were ties of friendship between them and Baldwin had a sense of honour. In his view, MacDonald had sacrificed his party in 1931 by continuing as Prime Minister, and deserved to be treated with respect even when he was an object of pity.

Younger men on the government side were impatient for a change at the top, and felt that the administration was suffering from a malaise. The Cabinet was in an overwhelming majority, opposed only by a weak opposition, and this bred complacency. There was a need for fresh faces, and Baldwin favoured a smaller team of ministers. But any reconstruction was difficult to effect as long as the Prime Minister remained. Up-and-coming Tories such as Macmillan were attracted by the idea of bringing in Lloyd George, for they welcomed the prospect of including someone in the government who had positive ideas. Chamberlain was doubtful about the feasibility of the Welshman's ambitious plans and thought his own were more likely to work. However, Baldwin was unenthusiastic; he still viewed Lloyd George as a showman, who would be 'not a cohesive, but a disintegrating force'.

In May, MacDonald finally announced his resignation. On 7 June Baldwin exchanged offices. Baldwin was the obvious successor as far as the King was concerned, but it would probably have been the wish of many Conservatives in the Cabinet and on the back benches to have had a change of leadership. Baldwin was recognised as an improvement upon MacDonald and he had a reputation then unequalled in British politics. They knew that he was a man who could handle the big occasion. But he was not likely to ignite their enthusiasm.

However, in the circumstances, there was no one willing to make a challenge. Neville Chamberlain did not push his own claims, though even MacDonald had assumed for much of his premiership that he and Baldwin would retire at the same time and that the Chancellor would take over. So Baldwin slipped back into the leadership for the third time, without his party ever being consulted. Chamberlain continued as Chancellor, Sir Samuel Hoare became Foreign Secretary, and the young Anthony Eden joined the Cabinet in a non-departmental capacity – with special responsibility for League of Nations affairs. Churchill was excluded, the wounds he had inflicted over India still being too recent a memory in Baldwin's mind for him to be forgiven.

On taking over, the new Prime Minister thought in terms of serving for two years, for 'I think by then I shall have given out all I have to give, and I should like to retire whilst still in possession of such faculties as I have'. He was aware of the difficult international situation, and saw that rearmament was going to be necessary if Britain was to 'speak with the voice we should, in favour of that collective security which is gradually commending itself to the people of this country'.

THE 1935 ELECTION

Baldwin's immediate task was to prepare for the forthcoming election, and he felt that one reason for an early ballot was to secure a mandate for rearmament. Churchill, having written in July in conciliatory terms to Baldwin, urged him of the need to 'go to the country at the earliest moment' with the same consideration in mind. He even promised his support for the Prime Minister in the election, believing that 'things are in such a state that it is a blessing to have at the head of affairs a man whom people will rally round'. Baldwin accepted his help, but he was an experienced campaigner in his own right. He was a shrewd electioneer, effective at exploiting Labour's deficiencies and maximising the government's own achievements. He was by then experienced in handling the voters, and he inspired trust among many of them.

The Prime Minister appreciated that 'the developments of the international situation' made an election desirable. Chamberlain agreed, saying that 'We are in for a long and anxious period of foreign affairs, in which it is essential that we should have a Government with the authority of the nation behind it.' The autumn was duly selected. The appeal Baldwin made was a strong one, for the government appeared to be well in control of events, and the ministerial team had the look of experience about it. Economic recovery was at last underway, house-building was booming and the pledge to tackle the areas still hit by the ravages of depression carried some weight. The other parties, by comparison, made little impact with their campaigning.

In the November election, Baldwin pitched his message to those people who wanted peace but believed that modest rearmament was a wise precaution. He was comfortable with such a stance which seemed likely to attract support from his natural constituency, Middle England. He had reason for optimism for with the possibility of looming international strife, he believed that voters would feel more secure with familiar faces in charge rather than those of an untried and inexperienced Opposition. In several speeches he dwelt on defence and the role of the League. He earnestly wanted peace and spoke of the need to maintain it, and in the light of later criticisms of his remarks concerning this election it is worth remembering that his other comments in the campaign were often clearly in favour of appropriate defence: 'The defence forces of the country must be brought up to such a state of efficiency that we may be able to make our proper contribution in the cause of collective security.'

As polling drew nearer, however, Baldwin emphasised peace rather than rearmament and his speeches struck just the right note for his audiences. Speaking to the International Peace Society, in a remark of calculated ambiguity, he observed 'that there will be no great armaments'. He also referred in characteristic terms to 'this dear, dear land of ours', after a passage in which he dwelt on the horrors of war and what it had meant to the British people:

> We live under the shadow of the last War and its memories still sicken us. We remember what modern warfare is, with no glory in it but the heroism of man. Have you thought what it has meant to the world to have had that swathe of death cut through the loveliest and best of our contemporaries, how public life has suffered because those who would have been ready to take over from our tired and disillusioned generation are not there?

He went on to spell out some of the joys of the British way of life, and spoke with feeling of 'the level evening sun over an English meadow, with the rooks tumbling noisily home into the elms . . . To what risks do we expose our treasures . . . Make no mistake; every piece of all the life that we and our fathers have made in this land, every thing we have and hold and cherish, is in jeopardy in this great issue.' One opponent on the political left was moved to a flight of fancy by the speech, labelling it 'the greatest speech a Prime Minister has ever made'. Neville Chamberlain, not always sympathetic to Baldwin's more leisured approach to the conduct of affairs, nonetheless wrote that: 'I will frankly confess that at times I have felt some transient impatience when it has seemed difficult to bring your thoughts down to the earthly decision I wanted. But when I read a speech like that, I can only think of our good fortune in having a leader who can raise us so far above ourselves, and can express what we should like to believe we had thought ourselves, in such moving words.'

It was one of Baldwin's finest performances, and one which made a greater than usual impact for a political speech. It seemed to be a statement of the inner thinking of a wise old statesman who had learnt a thing or two about the things that he and other people really cared about. Its delivery was a key point in the campaign, for whereas he gave several electioneering addresses this one had an altogether more reflective tone.

This was Baldwin's tenth election, the fifth and last he fought as leader, and his reputation stood him in good stead. Personally unopposed at Bewdley, he led the National Government to a massive victory, winning an overall majority of 247 seats. Inevitably, many constituencies were lost, for the 1931 result had been achieved under unusually favourable circumstances. However, he still had the second largest majority of the twentieth century. The glow of electoral success was soon to be dimmed (if not altogether extinguished) by his handling of events in Abyssinia.

FOREIGN POLICY – EARLY DEVELOPMENTS

Baldwin had taken over the premiership in the same month as the League of Nations Union had held the Peace Ballot (see page 104–5). Sir Samuel Hoare was his new Foreign Secretary, and was therefore responsible for the thrust of British policy after June 1935. Faced with the challenge of Hitler's aggression, British policy was to prove inconsistent. One policy was to work with France and Italy in an alliance to check German aggression. This had worked when Hitler threatened to absorb Austria into Germany in December 1934, and was formalised by the Stresa Front, an agreement of April 1935.

The alternative was to rely on collective security via the League of Nations, the policy for which the Peace Ballot indicated strong public support. The two policies were at variance, for Mussolini had already shown that he was intent on taking over the whole of Abyssinia. In August, Hoare had spoken in favour of sanctions against the Italians and on 12 September he showed strong support for the Covenant of the League of Nations and collective security: 'The League stands, and my country stands with it, for collective maintenance of the Covenant in its entirety, and in particular for steady and collective resistance to all acts of unprovoked aggression.' It soon became clear, however, that Britain could not and would not act alone on behalf of the League but it seemed that the Stresa option had also been dropped. Indeed, the Anglo-German Naval Agreement, which allowed Germany to maintain a navy of 35 per cent of the strength of the British one, was a flat violation of the Stresa Agreement – as well as the Treaty of Versailles. This gave out confusing signals.

Despite Hoare's protestations, the British reaction to Italian aggression over Abyssinia was unconvincing, for from the first the government was inclined to compromise.

ABYSSINIA AND THE INVASION OF THE RHINELAND

Italy's ambitions with regard to Abyssinia had been evident since December 1934 when, following a border incident, the latter had appealed to the League for help. Mussolini did not anticipate much opposition from other colonial countries such as Britain and France, and began to make active preparations to take control of Abyssinia. Britain was keen to see a compromise, and drew up proposals for a form of partition. However, with the election looming, the government simply expressed support for the League. Any response to aggression had to be collective, for there was no question of Britain acting alone.

To many Conservatives, the fate of Abyssinia was no big issue. Churchill's opinion was that it was difficult to view the country as a 'fit, worthy and equal member of a league of civilised nations' and he wrote off Mussolini's designs as 'a very small matter'. But ministers were aware that popular feeling in the country was less accommodating to the dictator, and this meant that the government had to move warily. Hence the resolute views expressed by Hoare about 'steady and collective resistance' in the face of unprovoked aggression, via the League.

Hoare's rhetoric seemed to indicate a strong commitment, and as the minister responsible for League affairs, Eden was surprised by his remarks. Hoare had struck a more realistic note when he had warned his colleagues that they could find themselves in 'a very inconvenient dilemma'. They might have to choose between 'a futile protest, which would irritate Mussolini and perhaps drive him out of the League into the arms of Germany, or we should make no protest at all and give the appearance of pusillanimity'. However, his speech of 12 September seemed to indicate that he was ready to use force, in concert with other members of the League.

The outcome of the Peace Ballot (made known in June) may have helped to swing Hoare's feelings, for there was every indication that the public wanted to see sanctions against the aggressor. Baldwin was conscious of this popular mood, and the two men had agreed on a firm approach although many colleagues were surprised by, and apprehensive about, the scale of the undertakings Hoare had given.

On 3 October 1935, Mussolini's troops invaded Abyssinia and four days later Britain secured a resolution branding Italy as the aggressor. Economic sanctions were imposed on 18 November, although the exclusion of oil limited their effectiveness. The government hoped that non-oil sanctions alone would force Mussolini to back down. It feared that sterner measures would increase Italian belligerence, and anyway there was doubt if they could be enforced. Weak sanctions, however, served neither to conciliate the Italians nor to stop them.

The Foreign Secretary met the French Prime Minister and Foreign Secretary, Pierre Laval, in Paris, in early December. A plan had been conceived to appease Mussolini by allowing the Italians to gain a large part of Abyssinia, with Abyssinia receiving a small part of Somaliland as compensation. The Emperor, Haile Selassie, would thus be able to retain his title, though he would rule over a small fragment of his territory. France was keen to settle along these lines, and revert to cooperation with Italy via the Stresa Agreement. Laval was in contact with Mussolini during the discussions in Paris.

The plan suffered when it was leaked in its formative stages on 9 December. The reaction in Britain – at Westminster and in the country at large – was immediately hostile, for it came too soon after an election fought by the Conservatives in support of the League. Public feeling had built up in support of Haile Selassie's position, and expectations had been raised by Hoare's remarks in early September. Many people were appalled by the Italian invasion and by the fact that ministers seemed now to be willing to condone Mussolini's behaviour and do a deal; they were not prepared for a ministerial volte-face.

Opinion in the Conservative Party soon became hostile to the Hoare-Laval agreement, for MPs began to note the critical response of their constituents. They were only too aware that their party had in the recent election pledged its support for the League as 'the keystone of British foreign policy', and 59 backbenchers signed a motion of disapproval of Hoare's action. Austen Chamberlain, who had largely vanished from the political scene, emerged from the background to articulate the discontent felt in the 1922 Committee and in the country at large. It seemed inevitable that the party revolt would bring Hoare down. Initially, Baldwin defended his Foreign Secretary, but it soon became clear that he must be sacrificed if the government was to survive. The proposal was dropped and Hoare was replaced by Eden.

The Hoare-Laval episode was a dreadful fiasco which greatly damaged Baldwin's standing in the country. It exposed his willingness to sell out the Abyssinians, which offended liberal opinion, and his own colleagues, whose policy he had been happy to endorse. When the going got tough, it was clearly time for the Prime Minister to let the Foreign Secretary get going.

Such conduct was highly damaging to Baldwin's personal reputation. With talk of an alternative government in the air, some considered it appropriate for Baldwin to resign. As the Labour leader, Attlee, argued, the 'honour of the Prime Minister' was involved, for he had 'won an election on one policy and immediately after victory was prepared to carry out another . . . [it has[an ugly look'. For a statesman who claimed to be a man of principle whom the public could trust for his decency and common sense, such behaviour seemed dishonourable.

Baldwin sought to defend the government's handling of events in a speech to the House of Commons, and for once he gave a lamentable performance. Hoare offered a successful defence of what he had done, stressing the practical realities of Britain's position; he retired with dignity, in spite of his partial responsibility for what had happened. By comparison, Baldwin's own contribution was less eloquent and convincing – in G. M. Young's phrase, 'feeble, toneless and unhappy'. He suggested that he was not yet in a position to reveal all the facts which, if only they were known, would ensure that 'not a Member would go into the lobby against us'. His lips were 'not yet unsealed' on the subject. Here, he was alluding to his suspicions that, as he later wrote, 'Laval had been bought by Mussolini'. A Secret Service report at the time showed that money had actually changed hands. But to show that Laval had literally 'sold out' to the Italians would have been to antagonise the French more than seemed wise in the international situation, so Baldwin felt it best not to reveal his suspicions.

Baldwin went on to admit that he should not have let a sick man (Hoare) go to Paris, and that the Foreign Secretary's proposals had gone too far. Neither would he fly in the face of public opinion and attempt to resurrect any aspect of them. The House accepted his apology, but it was a strangely ill-at-ease Prime Minister who addressed it that day. Austen Chamberlain was aware that, if he had chosen to 'put the boot in', he could have brought about his resignation, following 'a miserably inadequate speech and the initial blunder'.

The Hoare-Laval episode had been a shabby ploy to abandon Abyssinia, and the intensity of the reaction took Baldwin and his colleagues by surprise. His government had been given a severe jolt within a month of the election, and it was fortunate for him that the opposition had focused on Austen Chamberlain rather than Churchill, for Chamberlain was not the man to go for the jugular. Cartoonists were not to forget the episode, and for some while afterwards Low always portrayed Baldwin with sticking-plaster across his mouth.

Abyssinia was an issue over which Baldwin had given no clear lead, for his own thinking was very confused. He was alarmed by Mussolini's seeming determination to use force in pursuit of his aims, but, with other questions occupying his attention, he left matters largely to his Foreign Secretary and to Eden, both of whom were clearly sympathetic to the League. Neville Chamberlain, who was taking an increasingly important role in all Cabinet decisions, was also in favour of energetic action in pursuit of collective security, and sceptical of any formulae or deals. The Prime Minister recognised the limitations of Britain's ability to face any challenge by the Italian government, but did not try to cool expectations of a vigorous response should the need arise. In this situation, a climbdown was inevitable if the worst happened, and it did.

As Prime Minister, Baldwin must ultimately be held responsible for the policy pursued. In 1935, he had seemed to be committed to the resistance of aggression through the collective security provided by the League of Nations. However, the government was unwilling to make it a reality, and from a moral standpoint, its policy can be condemned on two counts. Firstly, by its refusal to impose oil sanctions, which would have helped to bring Mussolini into line. Secondly, by the Hoare-Laval Pact which seemed to be a particularly shoddy agreement. The contrast between the pre-election and the post-election positions was marked, and appeared to suggest that ministers were content to give a misleading impression of what they were willing to do in order to court the popularity of the voters. The policy was at best feeble, at worse cynical and opportunist.

In the event, economic action did not deter Mussolini who achieved complete victory in May 1936, when Abyssinia was annexed. Sanctions had been effectively abandoned early that year, and by June they were formally ended; in Chamberlain's words, they had become 'the very midsummer of madness'. Before they were finally dropped, however, Germany had struck another blow to the policy of collective security.

On 7 March 1936, Hitler sent troops into the Rhineland, an area demilitarised by the Treaty of Versailles. Many people in Britain had come to believe that the Germans had been harshly treated in 1919 and so it as easy for the government to find reasons for inaction when the gauntlet was thrown down. It was said that Germany was only marching 'into its own back garden', and in any case Britain was in no position to employ military force; neither were the French looking for a fight.

Eden favoured some kind of negotiation, to bring about a token reduction of German troops or some other form of concession. Most members of the Cabinet inclined to Chamberlain's distrust of the French and his view that Germany might retaliate. For Baldwin, stunned by how wrong the Abyssinian episode had gone, there was no question of any concerted Anglo-French move. Any military action was inappropriate, 'out of proportion to what Germany had done'. No action was taken.

It may be that Hitler could have been stopped in his tracks in 1936 as Mowat has suggested: 'Strong action against Italy in December 1935 or against Germany in March 1936 might have prevented the Second World War.' Certainly, the failure to react more positively to the Rhineland invasion has been portrayed by some historians as the time when it became apparent that Britain was unwilling to act against aggression. The German dictator drew appropriate conclusions – that whatever further expansionism he indulged in would meet with no firm response from the western powers.

Most evidence suggests that Mowat's scenario was unrealistic. Possibly the Germans would have withdrawn if faced with a show of strength, but there was never much likelihood that the French would have adopted such a policy, even though the Rhineland was adjacent to their border. They were unwilling, and rapid Anglo-French cooperation was unlikely at that stage. The British would not act alone, for the stakes were too high. To have unilaterally resisted over the Abyssinian question would have been risky, but might have had a chance of success. To have resisted over the Rhineland would have been more hazardous, for if Germany had decided to face the threat rather than back down it might have been victorious.

The fear was that in 1935–6 the German military was sufficiently well-equipped to have overwhelmed even Britain and France acting in unison. Britain on its own would have been no match for the Germans. The perils of a display of strength were too dangerous. Middlemas and Barnes have suggested that 'two things are essential to a nation going to war – public support and military strength. Britain had neither.' The comment points to Britain's military weakness, and Baldwin was aware that rearmament was needed. There might come a point when resistance would be necessary, but until the country's defences were stronger Britain could not afford to act. It is to that question of rearmament that we must shortly turn.

One final point concerning the events of 1935–6 is worth making at this stage. The failure of effective collective action at that time further undermined faith in the League of Nations, the authority of which was shattered. British policy had done little to assist its reputation, and the truth was that many Conservatives were not unduly concerned about this. The concept of action through some international machinery was alien to the way in which they viewed world affairs. Many of them preferred to see foreign policy conducted on the basis of national interest, irrespective of the wishes of some international body. In this view, the aspirations and interests of individual states were best reconciled through diplomacy – the idea of international peace-keeping was unrealistic. But the peculiar horror of the First World War, with its appalling slaughter, had led even them into thinking that some new system of international relations was desirable, and the League had been the embodiment of that idea. Lindsay and Harrington put the point well: 'The Conservative Party . . . was caught up in a movement of opinion which was hostile to its instinctive convictions. Thus it is not surprising that Conservative politicians, in office, should have betrayed an uncertain touch and an ambiguous attitude towards the League and collective security. On the one hand, it can certainly be maintained that the Conservative government of the 1930s contributed to the failure of collective security. On the other hand, it can equally be maintained that the idea of collective security, and the political weight behind it, corrupted Conservative thinking and prevented a successful and consistent Conservative foreign policy'.

REARMAMENT

It is over rearmament and the question of Britain's military preparedness that Baldwin's reputation has been most assaulted. The National Government had abandoned the Ten Year Rule in 1932, and the collapse of the Disarmament Conference and reports of German rearmament prompted a reassessment of Britain's position. Defence estimates were at a low point in 1932, and in 1934 Churchill claimed that Britain was only the fifth world power. In response, Baldwin promised that ministers would ensure that 'in air strength and air power this country shall no longer be in a position inferior to any country within striking distance of our shores'. He actually cared more about rearmament than the remarks of his critics suggest: 'A country which shows itself unwilling to make what necessary preparations are recognisable for its own defence will never have force – moral or material – in this world.'

By November 1934, when Churchill suggested that Britain's air power was being overtaken by that of Germany, Baldwin still took the view that it was untrue that Hitler's force was reaching equality with Britain's own: 'Our estimate is that we shall still have a margin in Europe alone of nearly 50 per cent.' In March 1935 a 'Statement Relating to Defence' was produced, in which rearmament was stated to be necessary. Air estimates were increased, and prototypes of the Hurricane and Spitfire were to be constructed. But with an election looming, there was no great emphasis upon further military preparations.

We have seen that during the election Baldwin pledged his full support for the League and collective security, though he had once thought them 'hardly worth considering'. He handled issues with some skill, stressing that there would be 'no great armaments' but that the government would 'provide adequately for our country's safety . . . Beyond that point it is not intended to go.' Rearmament was downplayed, and in his election broadcast, he spoke of 'repairing gaps'. Even so, he was accused by Labour of warmongering. Attlee was sharply critical of ministers: 'What they really want is big armaments in order to play the old game of power politics.' Neville Chamberlain had been keen to fight the election on rearmament and foreign policy, his reasons having more to do with party than national considerations; he saw the topic as being one on which the Opposition was vulnerable.

After the election, rearmament became more open. In March 1936, a White Paper was produced, and there was growing pressure for the appointment of a Minister of Defence, as an indication of increased commitment. Churchill would have liked the role, but his hopes were dashed. Instead, a less exalted appointment was made to a less exalted office. Sir Thomas Inskip became Minister for the Coordination of Defence. It was not a happy choice, for Inskip was an unsuccessful minister. Moreover Baldwin had delivered a slight to Churchill which may account for the sharper tone of his subsequent criticism.

Churchill was a member of a delegation which went to see the Prime Minister to make representations on the need for rearmament, in July 1936. The delegation contained a number of other eminent men in the Conservative Party, including Austen Chamberlain and Lord Salisbury. However, it was Churchill who presented the cases, and for over an hour he addressed Baldwin and Inskip. Other speakers pressed the argument over two days, and Baldwin was made well aware of the growing feeling within the party that action was needed sooner rather than later.

It was in a debate in November 1936 that Churchill accused Baldwin of sloth in rearmament, and went on to make a sweeping assault on Britain's inadequate air defence:

> The Government simply cannot make up their minds, or they cannot get the Prime Minister to make up his mind. So they go in strange paradox, decided only to be undecided, resolved to be irresolute, adamant for drift, solid for fluidity, all-powerful to be impotent. So we go on preparing more months and years – precious, perhaps vital, to the greatness of Britain – for the locusts to eat.

Baldwin responded by describing the approach of all parties in the 1920s to issues of defence, and pointing out that Churchill, as Chancellor, had been as much involved in defence cuts as any one else in the Cabinet: 'We did it because we still had hopes of disarmament, because we believed that there was no danger of a major war within a decade and because we were anxious to conserve the finance of the country.' The difference between him and Churchill over rearmament, he continued, began only in 1933, and here it was important to realise that 'a democracy is always two years behind the dictator'. He conceded that the government had also been convinced of the need for rearmament since 1933, but had preferred to proceed by persuading people of the necessity to act. He added:

> Supposing I had gone to the country and said that Germany was rearming and we must rearm? Does anyone think that this pacific democracy would have rallied to that cry at that moment? I cannot think of anything that would have made the loss of that election from my point of view more certain.

It was this extract which was to be quoted and misquoted for several years after, although the whole speech has been criticised. It was received with what the *Annual Register* called 'raised eyebrows'. There was deep shock at Westminster, partially at the way in which the remarks were delivered, but more especially at their content. Harold Nicolson described the performance as that of a 'tired walker on a long road . . . The House realises that the dear old man has come to the end of his vitality.'

Critics seized upon the passage quoted above. G. M. Young was to observe that: 'Never I suppose in our history has a statesman used a phrase so fatal to his own good name and at the same time, so wholly unnecessary, so incomprehensible.' By selective quotation, it could be interpreted to mean that Baldwin's primary concern was not the national interest, but the desire to win the 1935 election, and for this reason he had kept rearmament out of the campaign. As such, it seemed to indicate an utterly opportunistic approach to the conduct of affairs.

Baldwin's meaning was misinterpreted for he was speaking of the East Fulham by-election, as a reading of the whole speech makes clear. Rearmament certainly did not figure prominently and no attempt was made to warn people of its inevitability. But all that he actually said was that a by-election fought on rearmament would have resulted in a Conservative defeat which would not have helped the cause. As Rhode James observes: 'As a statement of historical fact, it was incontrovertible.'

Churchill exploited Baldwin's remark as though it was a new and startling insight into the Prime Minister's attitude, although he had heard Baldwin speak similarly on previous occasions, particularly at the time of the July delegation. It provided him with the basis of his later assault on Baldwin. He accused him of deceiving the electorate, and in a damning index reference in the first volume of his history of the Second World War, *The Gathering Storm*, he wrote that 'Baldwin, Stanley, confesses to putting party before country'. The charge was elaborated and reiterated for a long while afterwards, and Churchill tried to show how calculating Baldwin had been in 1935:

> Having gained all that there was in sight upon a programme of sanctions and rearmament, he became very anxious to comfort the professional peace-loving elements in the nation, and allay any fears in their breasts which his talk about naval requirements might have caused . . . Thus the votes both of those who sought to see the

nation prepare itself against the dangers of the future, and of those who believed that peace could be preserved by praising its virtues, were gained.

In *Guilty Men*, a left-wing tract written by Cato (Michael Foot and others) in 1940, the indictment was most boldly made, for the implication was that the government was sympathetic to fascist dictators and sought to accommodate them.

The charge of putting party before country was unfair but Baldwin was certainly slow to take up the cause of rearmament and place British forces in a state of adequate preparedness. His mandate came two years later than he himself admitted was desirable, and then he was still slow to move. Perhaps he was still unclear as to how much support there was for rearmament, and whether he did really have a mandate. Certainly, he had done nothing to convince the Opposition, Parliament or the country at large.

Rearmament did proceed but there was no sense of urgency. Expenditure rose from £137,000,000 in 1935–6 to £186,000,000 a year later, and £198,000,000 in 1937–8, but the years 1936–8 were an era of wishful thinking. In the autumn, Chamberlain could state frankly that 'progress is not yet as fast as I should like. Better than France, behind Germany and falling further behind.'

In their reluctance to press ahead with rearmament, ministers had the backing of the Left for when measures were announced in March 1935 Attlee made it clear that: 'We believe that the policy here outlined is disastrous.' But he did not have the responsibility of office. Neither did other voices which opposed increased expenditure on national defence. It was this point that was made by the editor of *The Times* on Baldwin's death: 'Democratic leadership demanded that he should go to the country with a frank acknowledgement of the dangers, challenging its illusion with inconvenient truth and risking defeat.' The charge may have been inapplicable to the election of 1935, but the criticism of unwillingness to give an appropriate lead is one that Baldwin's defenders have found difficult to deny.

EVENTS IN SPAIN

In early 1937, the Germans and the Italians combined in a further demonstration of military power. The Spanish Civil War had broken out in July 1936, when General Franco's nationalist forces crossed from Morocco into Spain in rebellion against the republican government. What seemed at first like a straightforward coup flared into a brutal civil war, conducted with great ferocity on either side. It became a major international issue, and was to be portrayed as a struggle between the forces of democracy and those of fascist aggression. Hitler and Mussolini sent troops in support of Franco's fascist rebels and their monarchical supporters, whilst the Russians assisted those Spaniards loyal to the government.

Britain urged the powers to join a Non-Intervention Committee which agreed that no military assistance be given to either republican or nationalist forces. The effect was to deny the former any chance to buy arms at the same time as the nationalists were gaining powerful reinforcements – for Italy and Germany were only too happy to use Spain as a training-ground for their arms and men.

It was difficult for ministers to hold the line, for theirs seemed an unheroic stance which was beneficial only to the aggressor. But opinion in the country was divided, and Baldwin was fearful of adopting the policies of one side and alienating those who took a different view. As he put it: 'There was one thing more than anything that I was afraid of – party division on foreign policy.' Spain threatened both party and national unity, and one of his fellow-Conservatives expressed this anxiety clearly:

> In this country at all times, but especially at the present juncture, when the whole energy of the state is required to unite reasonable men in defence of our existing institutions . . . it is of the greatest moment that the public sentiment should not be distracted or divided by an unnecessary interference of the Government in events passing abroad over which they have no, or at best very imperfect, control.

There was an element in the Conservative Party which was sympathetic to authoritarian regimes and leaders abroad. In some cases, its adherents were anti-semitic, most were anti-Bolshevik and Hitler and Franco were viewed as a bulwark against international Communism. Churchill supported Franco as a sound bastion against the Red menace. Businessmen tended to agree and believed that Britain's economic interests required a victory for the nationalists. *The Times* also encouraged the policy of conciliating Hitler and the fascist powers.

On the left of the Conservative Party, some young Tories were angered by the supine approach to the would-be dictator. They rallied in support of the elected Spanish government, and a range of left-wing opinion in Britain, from Liberal readers of the *News Chronicle* to anarchists on the far Left, were pro-Republican. But it was difficult to secure unity for Attlee, as the leader of the main opposition party, was only interested in any kind of popular front if it was united on the basis of a socialist programme.

The struggle in Spain was widely portrayed as a contest between the forces of fascism and those of Communism. In actual fact, there were no Communists in the Spanish government and the Spanish fascists (Falangists) were only but a part of the coalition fighting under the nationalist banner. However, outside Spain, those who worried about the rise of fascism in Europe felt that the fight for democracy in Spain was a worthy cause, and the Labour Party urged pressure on Germany and Italy to abide by the policy of non-intervention – without any success.

Baldwin did not wish to involve himself in the issues but as Prime Minister the handling of Spanish problems, as with those of Abyssinia and the Rhineland, were ultimately his responsibility and history judges his performance accordingly. When he left office the divide over foreign policy issues was significantly hardening, and historians have spent much time debating the rights and wrongs of defence and foreign policy. However, it was the policy of appeasement associated primarily with Neville Chamberlain when he became Prime Minister in 1937 which has been the particular object of derision and revision. That policy had its origins in Baldwin's era, but it was Chamberlain who advocated and implemented it with more energetic determination. The latter died before the storm of criticism broke out over the conduct of foreign policy in the 1930s, and if much of the controversy concerned his role, he was not there to attack. Baldwin was, and therefore it was his alleged neglect which attracted particular opprobrium.

1936: A VERY BAD YEAR

In 1936, there were many who doubted the wisdom of Baldwin's return to the premiership a year earlier. He had his own misgivings also, and sank into even greater lethargy. He had exhausted his reserves of prestige, and his performances were greeted with a mixture of ridicule and dismay. It was Churchill who caught the prevailing mood in a cruel but memorable remark. At the time when Baldwin was seeking to appoint the Minister for the Coordination of Defence and was tardy in announcing his choice, Churchill had his own explanation for the delay: 'Baldwin has to find a man of inferior ability to himself, and this Herculean task requires time for its accomplishment.'

There were signs that Baldwin was going the way of MacDonald. He seemed increasingly decrepit, becoming notably deafer and lapsing into a state of nervous exhaustion. In the House of Commons he was often unable to hear his questioners and his speeches had become increasingly ineffective. His friend Davidson frankly confided: 'Every mongrel is yapping, believing that a very tired old fox has gone to ground at Chequers, with no fight left in him.' It seemed as if his career had run out of steam, and he appeared to be a rather pitiable figure. In spite of its majority, his government had lost the confidence of many MPs in the Chamber and many backbenchers on his own side were openly defiant. Over defence policy, he was fortunate that his critics were divided – for some Conservatives, the pace of rearmament was too slow, whilst on the Labour benches there were serious reservations about any rearmament at all.

But whatever the disagreements over policy, Baldwin's enemies could unite in denouncing the lack of effective leadership. Lloyd George observed ministers to be 'running away, brandishing their swords' and a Labour front bencher, Arthur Greenwood, spoke of a 'trembling, vacillating, cowardly government'. But again it was Churchill whose choice of language rubbed salt into the open wounds. He linked MacDonald and Baldwin together and accused them

> of excelling in the art of minimising political issues, of frustrating large schemes of change, of depressing the national temperature and reducing Parliament to a humdrum level . . . If the supreme need of John Bull after the war and its aftermath was a rest cure, no two nurses were better fitted to keep the silence around a darkened room and protect the patient from anything in the nature of mental stress or strong emotion.

Not surprisingly, Baldwin began to feel persecuted. His critics had plenty of ammunition – Abyssinia, the Hoare-Laval pact, the Rhineland, the war in Spain, the Inskip appointment – and used it to attack ministers relentlessly. He suspected a plot and that Churchill was involved in it. He told a surprised House of Commons that this was 'the time of year when midges come out of dirty ditches'. Baldwin was beginning to seem pathetic, as he looked around for people to blame. But there was one issue which, whilst contributing to his anxiety and nervous exhaustion, was soon to allow him to redeem his personal position. This was the affair which became known at the time as 'the King's Matter', but which we know better as the Abdication Crisis.

THE ABDICATION CRISIS

King George V had died in January 1936 and his own anxieties about his successor were soon to be shared by Baldwin and other senior ministers. They suspected that Edward's heart was not in the task and that whilst he enjoyed the privileges of kingship he was unwilling to exercise the necessary sense of responsibility and decorum. He had been a popular Prince of Wales, once appearing to show a genuine sympathy for the unemployed, but by the mid-1930s many in government viewed him as a shallow, self-indulgent figure attracted primarily by the glamour of his position.

Baldwin was apprehensive from the start and his forebodings were recorded by Thomas Jones on the first day of the new reign: 'SB is distinctly nervous about him.' The Prime Minister was only too aware of his responsibility of 'having to take charge of the Prince as King'. He personally liked Edward, and had commented on his 'flair for public and private sympathy' to those in need. As long as there was no question of marriage, he was watchful and anxious, but not unduly alarmed. There was a world of difference between the King's behaviour within his private social circle and his fitness to reign over the British people. Chamberlain was more offended by Edward's lifestyle and lack of moral rectitude, and saw him as at heart an indiscreet and extravagant socialite without the necessary qualities to rule: 'I do hope he pulls his socks up.'

Edward was still a bachelor at 41, and it was his relationship with one particular woman which was the main cause of much contemporary unease about his suitability for office. He was infatuated with an American divorcee, Mrs Wallis Simpson, and showed no sign of giving her up on assuming the crown. Baldwin and his colleagues already knew of the relationship, but it had been a delicate matter to discuss with the old King. To have agonised over the succession would have been to anticipate his death. In any case, Baldwin was not the man to take a needless or unforced initiative, even when he foresaw the prospect of possible trouble ahead.

In the summer of 1936, the relationship with Mrs Simpson was a common cause of gossip in London society, but there was no indication that Edward was contemplating marriage. She was at that time still married to her second husband, a London stockbroker, but as the consort of a king she had another disadvantage – she was a commoner. An American, a nobody (in society's terms) and a divorcee (about to divorce yet again) – these were formidable disadvantages for a would-be wife of an English sovereign. But Edward was unabashed at his relationship and openly flaunted it, happy to accompany her on many a public occasion.

In 1930 Edward had bought Fort Belvedere in Windsor Great Park to entertain Mrs Simpson, and he gave her expensive presents. The British press showed remarkable restraint in adhering to a voluntary agreement not to refer to the affair, but in Europe and America there was much speculation about the King's behaviour and intentions. When Baldwin returned from his annual holiday in October, he was made aware of the flood of letters at Number Ten concerning Edward's conduct as depicted in overseas newspapers. By then, the news had broken that the Simpson divorce case was to be heard in late October, and the prospect of a royal marriage seemed more imminent.

In theory, of course, the King could marry the woman of his choice, but marriage against the advice of his ministers was inconceivable for the crown would be placed in the middle of political controversy. Neither Baldwin nor any likely alternative leader would have agreed to serve as Prime Minister if the government's wishes had been flouted. In their reactions, all were aware that the Church of England (of which the monarch was the head) was opposed to divorce, as was a large segment of public opinion.

The Prime Minister was not unduly anguished by the impending crisis. He was now recovered from his earlier exhaustion, and felt more than able to cope with the situation. As long as crises did not occur with too much regularity, he could rise to the occasion. Moreover, this was a crisis of the type in which his qualities were likely to be supremely appropriate. It involved his ability to gauge the reaction of the general public and achieve a rapport with the popular mood – gifts with which he was generously endowed.

RIP STAN WINKLE RETURNS
(Mr. Baldwin returns to No. 10 Downing Street after a long period of rest)

Baldwin returns from a short break to face 'the King's Matter'.
Strube (Daily Express)

Baldwin was not unaware of the boost to his reputation which adroit handling of the situation could effect. Clearly, this was for him the matter on which he had to concentrate his attention. The marital problems of the King were less taxing, and probably more susceptible to a solution than were unemployment, rearmament and civil war in Spain, and he soon told his new Foreign Secretary, Sir Anthony Eden, that he must not be troubled with foreign affairs. Eden was surprised to hear this ('I found this an astonishing document'), for he had neither seen him nor received a communication on foreign affairs for three months, at a time when events in Spain were at a critical juncture.

Urged on by Geoffrey Dawson, the editor of *The Times*, Baldwin had his first discussion with the King. It was not an easy confrontation, but Baldwin had braced himself with whisky and soda before advising Edward that 'I don't believe you can go on like this and get away with it.' He suggested that the divorce be postponed, and that Mrs Simpson might move off-stage for a few months. No puritan himself, he would have preferred to see Edward behave as other monarchs had done before him, taking lovers but not marrying them. The King listened, but felt that the Simpsons' divorce was not a matter for him. In fact, shortly afterwards, a decree nisi was granted, and Edward hoped that a marriage might be possible before the coronation.

Baldwin was content to wait on events and let matters drift for a while. It was unlikely that the affair would fizzle out and Baldwin did not expect it to, but the respite gave the King the chance to reflect on the position in which he found himself. The Prime Minister knew the outcome he wanted and was prepared to be patient before bringing matters to a head and forcing a decision. As yet, he had not taken the whole Cabinet into his confidence, but Neville Chamberlain was fully in the picture. The latter drew up a memorandum for Baldwin to send to Edward. It amounted to a virtual ultimatum, and was illustrative of his approach to affairs. It was uncompromising, suggesting that the

> association with Mrs Simpson . . . be terminated forthwith – should this advice be rejected by Your Majesty, only one result could follow . . . that is the resignation of myself and the National Government. If Mrs Simpson left the country forthwith, this distasteful matter could be settled in a less formal manner.

As Roy Jenkins has remarked, 'Chamberlain obviously thought the King should be dealt with more like the Poplar Board of Guardians than like Hitler.' The memo indicated Chamberlain's view of the kind of behaviour that could be expected from the Crown Head of State. His sense of propriety was clearly offended by Edward's dress and manner, but also by his tendency to make comments which he felt were inappropriate for a Prince of Wales. Baldwin was altogether more emollient, and had no reason to give unnecessary offence. Moreover, any blatant discourtesy might have the effect of rallying opinion around the King.

At a second meeting a month later, the King enquired as to whether marriage between he and Mrs Simpson would be acceptable. Baldwin doubted that the country would approve, but did not reveal the collective thinking of ministers. When Edward declared that he would abdicate, Baldwin declined to comment specifically on this course of action, but remarked that he would be 'deeply grieved' if this should happen. Before the next meeting, there was talk of a morganatic marriage, by which Mrs Simpson could have become Edward's wife but not his Queen. The idea appealed to the King but not to Baldwin, and after consultation with the whole Cabinet and the Dominion prime ministers he killed the idea before it really got off the ground.

Events were moving to a conclusion. Baldwin was now fully aware of the seriousness of Edward's intentions, and was under some pressure from his Cabinet colleagues. He also recognised that undue delay might encourage support for the small King's Party in the House of Commons, for he might gain sympathy for his personal plight – caught as he was between his desire for the crown and his desire for his mistress to become his wife. Rothermere and Beaverbrook were drumming up support in the press, and Churchill, an ally of both the King and the institution was urging that Edward be given time to resolve his difficulties.

The King, who had once believed that he could separate his private life from his public role, now recognised the inevitability of his abdication in the face of unyielding pressure from his ministers. On the last occasion that he and Baldwin discussed the arrangements, they parted without evident bitterness, the Prime Minister wishing Edward 'happiness where you believe it to be found'. On 10 December, he went to the House of Commons to tell MPs of the King's decision. He was aware of the importance of the occasion, and his customary nervousness left him as he prepared himself for the task. He felt that he was the man for the occasion, and as he remarked: 'This is making history, and I am the only man who can do it.'

The speech, described as 'the quintessence of human artistry', was a parliamentary triumph. He spoke for the bulk of MPs on all sides in language which was not especially majestic, but which was nonetheless very moving. The remarks were not particularly well-organised, for Baldwin's notes had been accidentally knocked to the floor by a front bench colleague, and were scattered and ill-arranged. As the *Manchester Guardian* commented: 'With infinite daring, he spoke extempore from notes that always seemed to be in alarming disarray.'

The Prime Minister proceeded to give a full account of the unfolding story. He skilfully narrated the sequence of events to his rapt and solemn audience, and avoided speaking ill of any person involved. At each juncture in the story, he generously interpreted the King's behaviour, and as Middlemas and Barnes perceived, in so doing, 'lifted the crisis at last from rumour and scandal on to the high dramatic plane where it has since largely remained'.

Harold Nicolson realised that he had heard something remarkable, and described how 'we file out, broken in body and soul, conscious that we have heard the best speech that we shall ever hear in our lives . . . No man has ever dominated the House as he dominated it tonight, and he knows it.' Baldwin had indeed agreed with Nicolson that it was a success, and added: 'I had a success . . . at the moment I most needed it. Now is the time to go.' He had handled the affair in such a way that he earned plaudits from all around. The King even wrote of his 'characteristic humanity and understanding which helped to lighten some of the heaviness of those days', although later in retirement he struck a more embittered note.

Few other politicians could have equalled Baldwin's performance, for whereas Neville Chamberlain might have alienated the King and country, Churchill would have got the outcome wrong – but with some eloquence. In all essentials, Attlee was in agreement with the Prime Minister, but he lacked his rapport with the people which enabled him to 'speak for England'. Chamberlain recognised this facility, and wrote to his wife about it: 'SB, as I anticipated, has reaped a rich harvest of credit which has carried him to the highest pinnacle of his career.' The Chancellor acknowledged that Baldwin 'undoubtedly perceived and expressed the profound will of the nation'.

In later years, when Baldwin's reputation was much reviled, there was still a general acceptance that he had handled the Abdication Crisis well. Even G. M. Young, his less-than-friendly biographer, acknowledged the way in which Baldwin had held and retained the middle ground, neither antagonising the King nor weakening in his determination to achieve the outcome he favoured. He wrote: 'I am profoundly impressed by the simple skills SB displayed, making the outcome seem inevitable. It is like one of the great chess games – and yet only one man could have played it'. Young went on to quote Beaverbrook's observation, that Baldwin 'foreknew the abdication, just as he foreknew the general strike. If only he had turned his eye abroad, he would have foreknown the course of Hitler, and how to arrest it. But foreign voices had no meaning for him.'

If the latter part of the comment is rather unfair, nonetheless it makes a valid point about the amount of time consumed by the 'King's Matter'. It so occupied Baldwin's mind that he was distracted, not unhappily so, from more pressing issues abroad. In truth, the problem was a massive diversion for along with Baldwin, the British people also preferred to avert their gaze from the continent and absorb themselves in the doings

THE WORCESTERSHIRE LAD

Farmer Bull. "WELL DONE, STANLEY: A LONG DAY AND A RARE STRAIGHT FURROW."

Baldwin bows out in a glow of glory. (Punch-Mansell)

of the Royal Family. Nevertheless, the cost of Baldwin's involvement was great, for he was already under much pressure from the weight of the burdens upon him; by mid-1937, he was to be in a state of nervous exhaustion.

However, before the Prime Minister retired he was to render one last public service. This was to ensure the passage of the Ministers of the Crown Act which among other things raised MPs' salaries, for Baldwin realised that Labour members were at a disadvantage in that many of them lacked private means. In constitutional terms, its importance was greater, for it recognised for the first time the office of Prime Minister and Leader of the Opposition as official posts; for a long time, he had wished to see the status of the Opposition raised, by conferring payment on its leader. Both posts had been recognised in fact if not in law for many years, but in so regularising an existing situation, Baldwin bestowed a final service to democratic government to which he was deeply attached. Nicolson recognised the service, and wrote: 'So his final words are to give us all £200 a year more. This means a lot to the Labour members and was done with Baldwin's usual consummate good taste. No man has ever left in such a blaze of affection.'

ASSESSMENT OF BALDWIN'S THIRD PREMIERSHIP

In and after the Second World War it was to become fashionable to attack the governments of the 1930s, both for their failure to tackle unemployment at home and for the inadequacy of their handling of issues of defence and foreign policy. Baldwin's premiership was an important part of that decade, and he shares any blame which is attached to it.

In his defence, it may be said that Baldwin made some gesture towards rearmament, albeit without great urgency, and kept Britain aloof from wars on the continent – which is what most British people wanted. In the 1930s, politicians were faced by daunting challenges, and none of them had the answer to all of them. Even Lloyd George, who was ambitious and creative in his economic thinking, showed little understanding of the nature of the dictators who dominated the era. Baldwin was not indifferent to the threat they posed to national security, but was, like most of the others, incapable of devising a consistent and effective strategy with which to deal with them.

It had not been a very distinguished government over which Baldwin presided. He was still personally popular, and the House knew that he was capable of rising to the occasion as he did so effectively over the Abdication Crisis. But in other areas of policy, especially in defence and foreign affairs, there were blemishes on his record which created a less-than-heroic impression. The policies he adopted could be explained and even justified, but they did little to enhance his reputation. Those who admire Baldwin do so more because of his moderation and consensual approach at home than for his handling of overseas issues which so impinged upon his final performance on the stage of Ten Downing Street.

timeline	1935 May	Baldwin becomes Prime Minister again
	October	Italian invasion of Abyssinia
	November	Election victory
	December	Publication of Hoare-Laval Pact
	1936 January	Death of George V
	March	German invasion of Rhineland
	December	Abdication of Edward VIII
	1937 May	Retired

Points to Consider

1) 'The episode of the Hoare-Laval Pact was a shabby one from which Baldwin emerges with little credit.' Is this true?
2) 'Supine and ineffective.' Is this an appropriate phrase to sum up British handling of (a) the Abyssinian problem and (b) the invasion of the Rhineland?
3) How frank was Baldwin about the need for rearmament? Can he be defended against the allegation that he put 'party interests before those of the country' at the time of the 1935 general election?
4) 'Baldwin handled the Abdication Crisis superbly.' Which of his qualities enabled him to deal with the 'King's Matter' so successfully?
5) 'Like MacDonald, Baldwin remained at the helm for too long.' Does the record of Baldwin's third premiership suggest that this was true?

6

THE FINAL YEARS

Baldwin remained in office to see George VI crowned as the new king, but resigned shortly afterwards on 28 May 1937. He had planned the timing of his retirement with some care and he was aware that this was a good time to go. His handling of the Abdication Crisis was generally seen as a triumph, but to have departed immediately following his personal success might have been to quit at the wrong moment. By waiting for the coronation and seeing the new monarch firmly established, he could still depart in a glow of achievement and adulation, and take the credit for ensuring that there was a peaceful royal accession.

In the months before he left, Baldwin increasingly handed over control to his successor. No one doubted that Neville Chamberlain would replace him, and Baldwin was content to allow him to take charge to an ever greater degree. Defence and foreign affairs continued to arouse Prime Ministerial interest, but otherwise he tended to remain silent in Cabinet and the House when policy was discussed. When Tom Jones asked him what was to be done about Special Areas, the response indicated the lack of involvement: 'I don't know; I'm not on that committee.' Jones drew the conclusion that Baldwin was 'just caretaking' for Chamberlain, and was counting the hours to his retirement.

The Prime Minister's last speech to the House of Commons was characteristic, urging yet again the need for people to avoid the strife of industrial unrest and class conflict, and to remain wedded to the processes of peaceful and orderly change. He then left the Commons with the good wishes of MPs on all sides ringing in his ears, and in the speeches made to mark his resignation there was a genuine feeling of warmth and a note of sadness at the loss of such an esteemed Member. An editorial in *The Times* by Geoffrey Dawson expressed the hope that

'Freedom from the daily strains of party leadership will give him time and strength for those occasional utterances in which he has again and again, and never more than in these last few months, revealed himself as the authentic spokesman of the nation.'

Baldwin was the only prime minister to leave of his own volition in the years between the resignation of Lord Salisbury in 1902 and Harold Wilson, 74 years later. Others were sick, or were rejected by the electorate at an election or by their party in an atmosphere of jostling and conspiracy. His was an unforced exit. He was made a Knight of the Garter and within a few days was elevated to the House of Lords as Earl Baldwin of Bewdley. At his retirement, both in and out of the House, he was widely regarded with affection and few people voiced any criticism of him.

After his elevation to the Lords Baldwin played very little further part in public life. He had never had much affection or regard for Neville Chamberlain, but he recognised his dutiful service and did not wish to make his task as Prime Minister more difficult than it was already. He broadly supported the thrust of Chamberlain's appeasement policy, though it was pursued with more inflexibility than Baldwin would have attempted. He found himself in sympathy with Eden when the Foreign Secretary resigned in 1938 and was dismayed by Chamberlain's treatment of him. But Baldwin never stirred the cauldron from the House of Lords – he rarely attended its debates and his infrequent interventions were much less effective than his performances had once been.

Baldwin had doubts about the wisdom of the Munich policy, or more precisely about the way in which Chamberlain handled it. He would not himself have wanted Britain to fight on behalf of Czechoslovakia, but neither is it likely that he would have gone to meet Hitler. He was not optimistic about the chances of any lasting peace emerging from the Munich meeting, and as Middlemas and Barnes have summarised his attitude, he was 'half deploring the means, half praying for their success'. But in spite of his misgivings, he did not offer any public criticism. Referring to Munich in a speech to his fellow peers, he stated that 'I know that I could not have done it', but he chose not to elaborate on what his approach would have been.

Out of the political limelight, it might have been anticipated that Baldwin was set on course for a lengthy and fulfilling retirement. He had no money worries, he owned a substantial property in London and had as his family seat his beloved Astley Hall in Worcestershire. Baldwins Ltd was once again a flourishing concern, providing him with a very considerable annual income. His wife, to whom he was an affectionate and attentive husband, was still alive and his family were nearby.

Enjoying the esteem of his countrymen and with the opportunity to spend his time on the things he liked doing most, the future looked enticing. For a man who had always enjoyed his repose, a life of prolonged rest and leisure seemed the perfect recipe. Yet things did not work out as Baldwin had hoped. There were some attractive preoccupations. He had time to read the papers and his favourite books, he rediscovered his love of poetry, he listened to the wireless, he took occasional strolls in the countryside and he indulged his inclinations for eating, drinking, smoking and watching cricket. But in 1939, the peaceful England he loved became engulfed in a war which shattered that tranquillity which he sought in private and public life.

Baldwin's reputation was savaged when war came and he suffered much hurt from the assaults on his good name before he endured the other humiliation of being almost forgotten and ignored. He had viewed the prospect of war with mounting dread and when it came, the earlier displays of affection were cast aside and he was portrayed as the villain who had failed to prepare his country adequately for the hostilities. The nation needed a scapegoat and after Chamberlain's death in 1940, soon after his replacement by Churchill, Baldwin was the best available victim. When his name was recalled, it was often with abuse and references were usually highly unflattering. His mail included hate letters in which he was depicted as, at best, slothful but more often as the man who had deliberately misled or even betrayed his country.

Baldwin did not write his memoirs as many ex-politicians are wont to do, and because of this he lost the opportunity to tell events from his own perspective. As he lived through the devastating war which it was fashionable to believe could have been avoided by different diplomacy and a more vigorous policy of rearmament, the field was open to his critics to denounce his own role over the last decade. The letters and articles were venomous, and had started at the beginning of the war with an unfavourable review of his record in the *Sunday Express*:

It was on November 12, 1936, that Lord Baldwin, then plain Mister, arose in the House of Commons. He said he had not told the electors the truth about rearmament at the 1935 general election, because he believed that if he had done so they would not have voted for him.

Lord Baldwin did more damage to democracy than any other Premier in Britain, and certainly more damage than any other man except Cromwell.

The journalist involved provided much of the material for *Guilty Men* (see page 121), but it was a fellow scribe, 'Cassandra', in the *Daily Mirror*, who wrote a particularly waspish piece. Baldwin had shown reluctance to hand over the iron gates of his estate to the 'war effort'. The main ones had been presented to him to mark his retirement by the Worcester Conservative Association, while the rest were small and of limited value as war-time scrap, though they had a sentimental value, some being old, others having been especially commissioned. The council architect agreed that they were of artistic merit, and should be spared for they were fine examples of their type. But the matter was referred to higher authority, and in the event only the presentation set (the gates most suitable for conversion to steel) were left in place.

The affair created much publicity and had strange overtones. Beaverbrook was the Minister of Supply who had ordered the survey of wrought iron which could be used for war purposes. Later he admitted that he had pursued the requisitioning of Baldwin's gates with as much determination as he could. This was his revenge for the attack in 1931, for this time he had power as well as responsibility. During the affair, 'Cassandra' journeyed to Astley Hall to research the story. The readers of the *Mirror* learnt of 'the old and stupid politician who had tricked the nation into complacency about rearmament for fear of losing an election . . . the skeleton of our shady past . . . I want those gates to stay right there as a memorial and as a warning. I want them as a national monument to the attitude of mind that has put us in the desperate peril in which we now find ourselves . . . Here is the very shrine of stupidity.'

A. L. Rowse, in 1941, wrote an essay in which he reviewed the 'whole disastrous record' of Baldwin over 15 years. At the end he asked: 'What can the man think in the still watches of the night, when he contemplates the ordeal his country is going through as the result of the years, the locust years, in which he held power?' The charges went unanswered, perhaps out of a fear of stirring up division at a time when national unity was necessary. Baldwin knew he was a scapegoat and recognised that many people seemed to need one – he fulfilled that role and remained silent. Not until December 1944 did he finally yield to the advice of those relatives and acquaintances who felt that he should at least have his biography written so that his version of events might emerge: 'It would be some small comfort to see in writing the answers to these charges, and the truth, as I see it, set out, however long publication may be delayed.' His friend, G. M. Young was to be the author and Baldwin was never to know how the bonds of friendship were put aside as the historian wrote his inadequate and rather hostile account. The family were to be very disappointed with the outcome.

War inevitably altered Baldwin's personal life and though he was better placed than many people whose families were disrupted by separation and death, his home at Astley was no longer the peaceful haven of earlier years. Half of it was requisitioned for evacuees while he and his wife lived in the other half. The hall became increasingly decrepit as the war continued. Then, in 1945 Baldwin's wife died and his widowed eldest daughter came to keep house for him. Thereafter, his life lacked purpose and many of his last months were spent in arranging for the official biography to be written. He became a rather pitiable figure and at his last public function, was largely unrecognised. On 13 December 1947, Baldwin died in his sleep; his ashes were placed alongside those of his wife, under the nave of Worcester Cathedral. On his death there was no widespread mourning.

Political reputations come and go and Baldwin's has largely recovered from the dark days of the early 1940s when malice and spite were given free rein. His was an unusual experience, for whereas most politicians become venerated in old age as elder statesmen, it had been his fate to be reviled and treated with contempt. It was to be a generation or so before his reputation was re-assessed and his better qualities again accorded the recognition which was once so widely conceded.

timeline	1937 May	Retired
	1940	Publication of _Guilty Men_, and other attacks on Baldwin's premiership over alleged neglect of rearmament
	1944	G. M. Young chosen to write official biography
	1945	Death of Baldwin's wife
	1947	Death of Baldwin

A CONCLUDING ASSESSMENT

Baldwin's rise to political power had been a remarkable one. When he became Prime Minister he was associated with no famous issue or legislative achievement. Neither had he left any significant mark on any department. He was Prime Minister because no one better was available in 1923, a point which was recognised by the former Premier, Lord Rosebery, who observed that: 'It is a strange experience to realise that the Prime Minister of Great Britain is a man of whom one has never heard.' Yet over the next 14 years Baldwin became the most important politician of the age, and the man who stamped his imprint on the inter-war era – so much so, that the years from 1924–37 have become known as 'the Baldwin age'.

BALDWINIAN CONSERVATISM

Baldwin often expressed his belief in the traditional party preference for 'ordered liberty', in which people would hold their rights and obligations in an appropriate balance. Again, he was in the Conservative tradition when he emphasised a respect for the past, for proven methods and for the unchanging nature of human behaviour; hence, the attempt to establish some continuity in values and in practices.

Baldwin preached a simple patriotism, and set out to establish and maintain national unity. His general approach was accompanied by a broad and useful programme of social legislation. This was a brand of Conservatism which blurred the lines of class conflict and emphasised national interests and priorities, recalling Disraeli's idea of 'One Nation'; it enjoyed wide support in the community as a whole. In his wish to improve industrial relations and heal the wounds which open conflict sometimes brought about, his contribution was a lasting one.

The leadership of the Conservatives has often been more progressive than the rank and file. In Baldwin's case, this was conspicuously so. Whether in domestic political and social affairs, or in imperial and international ones, the Premier was well to the left of his party. He realised that it was necessary to do more than defend the existing order. He frequently made reference to Disraeli's fostering of social reform, and this provided the tone of his governments.

If Baldwin gave the people a vision of a more moderate Conservatism, it was as much due to his manner and approach as to his political ideas. He was no great thinker and his thoughts echoed those of many before. He had 'instincts and preferences, but nothing that could be called a political philosophy'. He imparted few new insights into the nature of Conservative ideas, but he provided the party with an approach that was more modern and humane as well as more electorally appealing.

FROM LAISSEZ-FAIRE TO COLLECTIVISM

In *Conservative Century*, Anthony Seddon has pointed to 1924 as a dividing line in Conservative history. From 1906–23 he argues that the party lacked a clear policy as well as being unable to achieve electoral success. None of its leaders – Balfour, Bonar Law, Austen Chamberlain or Baldwin – was able to inspire the party 'with a vision of modern Conservatism'. Baldwin had tried protection of home industry in 1923, and dropped it again quickly a year later. Thereafter, Seddon discerns a new phase in the party's history, and he describes the years 1924–40 as ones marked by 'the dominance of Baldwinian consensus . . . Baldwin . . . became the interwar party's chief architect, refashioning it after the hollow period that preceded it. The direction taken was towards pragmatic and selective state intervention in the economy and social policy.'

The distinction is a valid one and Baldwin did impart a new ethos and direction to Conservative policy after 1924. Unlike his predecessors who adopted a laissez-faire approach in which government intervention was shunned, Baldwin accepted that the government must step in and assume a new responsibility for the economy. He was not prepared to go as far along the road to state intervention as some politicians and economists were suggesting, but the creation of the BBC and the National Grid, and the derating of agriculture and the reduction of the rate burden on industry, were all symptomatic of the new willingness to embrace collectivist thinking, albeit of a limited kind.

Baldwin's approach, as his Conservative critics on the Right understood only too well, was to use the power of the state to tackle economic and social problems. The emphasis of his speeches was on a national response to national problems. This was far removed from the line taken by Conservatives in 1918–24, and quite unlike the style of Law, his immediate predecessor. Baldwin's governments prepared the way for the managed economy of post-1945 Britain, when it was accepted by all parties that ministers had a responsibility to use all their influence to tackle social and economic ills. This is why Lindsay and Harrington refer to him as 'the first of our collectivist Prime Ministers'.

CONSERVATIVE OPPOSITION

At times, Baldwin had to restrain the instincts of some of his more vengeful supporters who were more partisan than he was, and he was rarely free from the hostility of some MPs on his own back benches. His creed and style were anathema to the diehard section of his party which felt frustrated and thwarted by his attitude and actions. Its members despised his moderation, and felt particularly strongly about the menace of socialism – whilst he was willing to work with the emergent Labour Party. The more they attacked him, the more he increased his reputation with the Opposition.

G. M. Young has written of how 'throughout his public career, Baldwin was harassed by a group – always forming, always quelled, always re-forming – demanding [of him] something more than a continuous parade of good intentions garnished with quotations from Disraeli'. Yet for 14 years, in and out of office, he managed to retain the leadership of the party against supporters who were often impatient and clamouring for more distinctively Conservative policies. They wanted to see 'clear blue water' between their own policies and those of party opponents. At times, the dissidents almost had him 'on the run', and in 1924 his leadership was not terminated only because there was no obvious replacement who could command widespread assent. In 1931, as he put it, a faction was 'demanding [his] head on a charger'. But, he was not driven from office, as was Austen Chamberlain in 1922 or Neville Chamberlain in 1940, and was able to choose the moment of his own exit.

BALDWIN'S LEGACY

Overall, it is not just in his handling of particular issues that Baldwin's qualities must be judged. He had done something to raise the standards of integrity in public life. Men of greater ability and considerably greater dynamism may have been kept from the scene during the Baldwinian ascendancy, but the principles of decency, fairmindedness and attachment to democratic values had been kept in the foreground. There may well have been areas in which he failed to give a lead, and these failures could be exasperating to those with whom he worked. But his limited vision and drive can be viewed as a price worth paying for maintaining political freedom and stability at a time when events and upheavals elsewhere in Europe made stability an asset to cherish.

An indisputable achievement of British politicians between the wars is that they preserved their parliamentary institutions. Deeply attached to democracy, Baldwin made the democratic machinery work. The National Government might easily have been Britain's authoritarian response to the depression of the 1930s, but under Baldwin and MacDonald this was not to be. Like MacDonald, he consistently strove to guide his party towards the path of moderation and ensured that it remained there. Both leaders experienced setbacks but their complementary contributions in this respect were of lasting importance. The almost universal acceptance of methods of parliamentary government and the appreciation of the qualities which make it work owe much to the two men. This evolution is taken so much for granted that the commitment of those who helped to nurture it is often forgotten.

Baldwin was aware that there must be a balance between the demands of efficiency and social justice. It may well have been the case that stronger leadership would have resolved problems more efficaciously, but he understood the need for compromise, for winning people round and for acting in a spirit of responsible cooperation. He himself recognised that a more authoritarian approach might yield more dramatic results, as he indicated in a speech in 1934 on political freedom: 'I admit a dictator can do much. When in power he may do everything. But there is one thing he cannot do and that is create another dictator. Dictatorship is like a giant beech tree – very magnificent to look at it in its prime, but nothing grows underneath it.' His was a deep respect for democratic values, and it was maintained when other countries were abandoning their own.

The middle classes found Baldwin particularly reassuring and with the Conservatives so electorally successful they had little reason to turn elsewhere for political leadership. Baldwinian Conservatism was sufficiently all-embracing, pragmatic over policy and victorious at the polls that they could feel that their interests were suitably catered for. Continental creeds such as fascism made little impact on Britain, for the middle classes could feel safe and secure in the knowledge that there was an absence of deep social turbulence and unrest.

The dangers of class antipathy and social divisions had been reduced, and Baldwin helped to unite the nations behind his consensual policies. When he departed from the scene, the country was more 'at ease with itself' and, as war approached, could unite in the face of a common enemy that transcended any divisions at home. It was in no small measure due to Stanley Baldwin that such national harmony had been achieved. He was, as A. J. P Taylor has put it, 'a good man . . . [who] preserved and enhanced the civilised values that have distinguished British politics and the British people'.

Points to Consider

1) Baldwin's personality has been described as 'enigmatic'. Was he a more straightforward politician than some historians have led us to believe?
2) What were the more appealing characteristics of Baldwin's personality? What were its main deficiencies?
3) What were the strengths and weaknesses of Baldwin as (a) the leader of the Conservative Party and (b) Prime Minister?
4) Was it primarily because of Baldwin's popularity that the Conservatives were so electorally successful between the wars?
5) Is it fair to say that Baldwin was an appropriate Conservative leader and Prime Minister for the 1920s, but that his qualities were unsuitable to lead the party and the country in the more demanding days of the 1930s?

Index